ADELE BARLOW

LONG MAY YOU RUN

A GLOBAL NOMAD'S SEARCH FOR HOME

What happens when going 'home' makes you feel like even more of an outsider? When a Third Culture Kid (TCK) decides to move back to her passport country after university, she finds that 'homecoming' isn't straightforward when you've been raised around the world.

Designed to help TCKs struggling with where to go next, this thoughtful collection of original essays explores everything an international childhood brings. It also unpacks the question haunting many TCKs: where do you belong when you've grown up everywhere?

Eurasian writer Adele Barlow has contributed to TCK magazine *Denizen* and *The Huffington Post* among other publications. Having lived in Hong Kong, New Zealand, Malaysia and Australia, she is now based between London and Hong Kong.

To the expat kids, the internationals,
the ones who got moved around,
and now belong in the inbetween

TABLE OF CONTENTS

While all the stories in this book are true, some
names and identifying details have been changed
to protect the privacy of the people involved.

AUTHOR'S NOTE

WHAT IS A TCK, ANYWAY?

I T WAS THE START OF Form 2 (seventh grade) in Hong Kong. Our form teacher Mr. Goodman had asked us to write a short essay introducing ourselves. We had to include five fun facts that were about what made us unique. I couldn't wait to begin, and later, at home in my bedroom (where I had lobbied to put the prized family desktop computer), I furiously typed away on the black keyboard keys.

About an hour later, I leaned back from the looming wooden cage that housed the computer (IKEA's 'light pine computer stand') and proudly looked back over my work.

"What are you up to, darling?" Mum asked casually as she walked past my room on her way to the living room. I quickly looked at the piece and decided it was ready for an audience.

"Oh, just this *essay* for school," I said. It felt so grown-up to say that. Kids didn't write essays. *Teenagers* did. I was so close to being one. Although I wasn't too grown-up to tell Mum, "You can read it if you want."

She came into my room and started reading the piece over my shoulder. I couldn't wait to hear her feedback as I thought the essay had perfectly summed me up.

After a few minutes of silence, she made a funny noise that sounded like a sigh.

"Are you sure you want to include this?"

She pointed at a sentence on the screen from the opening paragraph, which proclaimed, "I like books and I have brown skin."

"How do you, ah, feel about your skin colour?" She asked. I shrugged. I didn't have feelings about it. I just wanted to add some physical description to the essay in case Mr Goodman didn't know who each of us was just yet.

I left the sentence as it was. The essay was perfect.

If I was going to write an essay introducing myself these days, I wish I had the confidence of my 12-year-old self. While I might not phrase things the same way, those two defining features haven't changed. What has changed is that over the twenty or so years between Form 2 and now, I've had plenty of time to think about the importance of books and skin colour.

I was born in Hong Kong to a Malaysian mother and a Kiwi father and went to a French school until I was 13. My family and I moved to Auckland, where I did high school, then I moved to Melbourne for university. That's where, while researching a sociology essay one afternoon in the campus library, I discovered the definitive book on Third Culture Kid living by David C. Pollock and Ruth Van Reken, along with this landmark quote:

"A Third Culture Kid (TCK) is a person who has spent a significant part of his or her developmental years outside the parents' culture. The TCK builds relationships to all of the cultures, while not having full ownership in any. Although elements from each culture are assimilated into the TCK's life experience, a sense of belonging is in relationship to others of similar background."

I was 17 at the time. When I found that TCK book, I felt like a light came on in a dark room I'd never really gone into inside my head. Finally, there was some explanation for something I'd been waiting for my whole life – there was a name for global nomads, who belonged everywhere and nowhere.

After stumbling upon this label, I read as many ideas as I could around the sociological and psychological aspects of growing up globally over the years to come. The official explanations have their purpose, but I craved reading about the inner lives of TCKs. I wanted to read the diary entries of others like me: were they as confused as I was about where they belonged? How did they find their place in the world?

I went on to write for an online TCK magazine in my early twenties and discovering other TCK writers there helped me see that I wasn't alone in my questions. I loved reading the confessions of others who had similar experiences: they had grown up on multiple continents, felt most at home in motion or in airports, and had been equally comforted by TCK writing.

At some point, I wanted to write a much longer piece, which I started but never finished (until now).

Now in my mid-thirties, this is my definition of how you know you're a TCK: you feel at home everywhere (on good days) and nowhere (on bad days). You feel connected to an international identity instead of a national one. You have friends from too many different countries to count (you've never even tried counting). When asked where you're from, you have multiple potential answers, depending on how much you feel like engaging with whoever's asking.

Looking back now, being a TCK never felt like a problem until I finished studying. That was when I got to decide where I got to live. Not my parents. Not my university. At those crossroads, I felt frozen.

When you can't make decisions, you get stuck. If you're too stuck for too long, you stop feeling anything. I thought depression was feeling sad. As it turns out, sadness means experiencing *something*: there are tears, feelings, release. Depression, however, is when you're wandering around an abyss, hoping to feel something, anything, ever again.

Perhaps you are facing similar challenges. Maybe up until now, a lot has been decided for you: where you go to school, and in turn, where you live. When you finish studying, there's no longer the expectation that you have to live in a specific place. That's when being a TCK can start to feel like an issue– if not here, then where do you go now?

After all, the places to which we belong are a core part of who we are and to be unsure of where we belong is to be uncertain of who we are. Since I was a teenager, my accent sometimes felt like it wasn't mine, my nationality was one I couldn't explain, and my passport linked me back to a country that felt like somewhere I was visiting as opposed to a place I was from.

I know I'm not the only TCK who has felt like this. We now live in an era where identity is constructed as opposed to inherited, so knowing where we belong has become more complicated.

I learned from these essays that home is a feeling and getting to that feeling is a transitional process. That transition can be blocked when your heart fears what your head is looking for. However, as I found through my time in Wellington, the process can be easier when you familiarise yourself with the psychological territory you are dealing with.

This is a collection of essays I started writing over a decade ago. I didn't release them for ages because they seemed sort of tone-deaf. *Oh, it's tough being an international jetsetter, huh?* That fear still lingers, and I think it's important to have a voice in your head that calls you out on your privilege (and your carbon footprint).

Yes, I know the TCK experience generally applies to a group with enough financial advantage to be globally mobile. I'm also aware that flying does our planet no favours. I also know that when you've grown up in multiple places, your mental health might have a layer that not all therapists recognise.

I am not a therapist, but therapy saved my life. It made me passionate about exploring the mental health obstacles TCKs can face. These hit me hardest when I finished university and moved back to my passport country of New Zealand. That's where this story begins.

[1]

BROKEN COMPASS

*"When you come out of the storm, you won't
be the same person who walked in.
That's what this storm's all about."*

\- HARUKI MURAKAMI

PART OF ME DID NOT want to be here, but here I was anyway. The *Jaws* theme song repeated in my head (*da-dum, da-dum*) as the faded metal elevator doors creaked open inside an office building in central Wellington. I stepped onto the floor and saw the glass door in front of me with the label I had been looking for. At the exact moment I reached for it, my hand on the cold metal of the handle, I wondered: was it too late to turn back now and pretend that I'd gotten lost? After all, this seemed a bit ridiculous. Why was I coming to see a *clinical psychologist*? What was even *wrong*? On the surface, nothing seemed broken, so I had no idea what I was here to 'fix'.

It was early October 2008. The world was excited about this senator from Chicago who could potentially be the first African-American elected president in U.S. history. This app called Facebook was starting to become a utility in our social lives, connecting us with friends we hadn't seen in years. iPhones had been released the previous year and seemed like the new futuristic, overpriced toys that everyone wanted but not many people had yet.

In my own little corner of the world, I had recently turned 22 and had graduated from Melbourne University earlier that year. After university, I had moved back to New Zealand to continue building a startup with my best friend and business partner, Pam, who I had met during high school.

We weren't going to be the next Zuckerberg, but thanks to what he'd achieved with Facebook, the climate for tech start-ups and young entrepreneurs was hyperactive, especially in America. We were in New Zealand but heard about people our age across the Pacific Ocean raising hundreds of thousands of dollars just for an idea. Over coffee in Auckland one day, Pam and I dreamed up an idea that went on to change both of our lives.

Our startup yMedia connected media students and graduates with community organisations that needed short-term digital volunteers. The students got much-needed work experience for their portfolios and the charities got free help navigating the online world. In our first year, we had pitched and won seed funding from one of the country's most successful entrepreneurs (Stephen Tindall, who started The Warehouse), attracted corporate sponsors like Microsoft and Saatchi & Saatchi, and grown a community of our own.

Running yMedia together had created a bond between us that felt more like a professional marriage. The startup was our baby, as well as a rollercoaster we were riding together, trying to figure out how much we could control and what was beyond anyone's influence. Yet I had underestimated how isolating running a startup could be, even when you were doing it with one of your best friends.

We had decided to move to Wellington for a fresh start. We'd started building yMedia in Auckland, but something about

'Windy Welly' felt more techie and interesting than the city in which we'd both completed high school. I also had a secret motive for moving to Welly: maybe it would be easier to feel 'at home' in a brand new city, and maybe that would make me feel more like a Kiwi, which I desperately wanted to be.

Yet as our first few months passed in Wellington, I started feeling haunted by a growing sense of worthlessness I had never experienced before. Pam - my closest and only friend in Wellington - had a new boyfriend, and as much as they were happy for me to tag along with them, I often felt like a third wheel. My parents lived a 12-hour flight away in Hong Kong, and for some reason, moving back to where they lived right then felt like defeat. My brother, who had always been my best friend, had just moved to London to start university.

I was living in a tiny room with a slanted roof on Pirie Street, in a dilapidated flat that Pam and I had stumbled across on TradeMe (NZ's equivalent of Craigslist). My housemates were three random guys a couple of years older, and we were friendly enough to have meals together a few times but were otherwise strangers. When I woke up each morning, I generally felt fine, but it was after work sometimes that I wondered: would anyone (besides Pam) miss me if I weren't here?

Did a bit of loneliness in a new place qualify me to go to therapy? What if the therapist heard me out and told me to leave her office because I was wasting her time? This ran through my mind as I gingerly sat in her empty waiting room, thumbing through an old *House & Garden* magazine. I was silently brainstorming excuses to leave without being rude.

While I couldn't see it at the time, the emotional architecture of my life was at a crossroads, leaving me feeling disconnected from everyone and everything. It was ironic to be holding that magazine because I feel like all I wanted with a deep desperation was to know where to find *my* house and my garden. I didn't even have to know which city. I'd settle for knowing on which continent I should be searching. Whenever I tried to read my inner compass, it felt broken.

At my core, I felt splintered. After growing up in Hong Kong then moving to Auckland for high school, then Melbourne for university, and now landing in Wellington, I felt so frustrated at *not knowing* where I wanted to place myself. I felt like the chapters of my life were scattered too far away from one another, that I was the only coherent thread between distant rooms in a house that felt too big and lonely.

On some level I had always felt torn between Asia and the West, but now, it was becoming harder to ignore. Like a splinter that turns into infection, something that had once seemed insignificant (my 'unplaceable' accent) had now become the bane of my existence.

Questions from people I met through friends or work had taken on a familiar pattern.

"Wait... you grew up there, but you're not *actually* from Hong Kong, right? Neither of your parents is Chinese, right?"

"Oh, your Mum's Malaysian? So you speak Malay?"

"So, where's home?"

"Where do you think you'll settle down eventually?"

They're just being friendly, I would tell myself. But I had become so secretly defensive about not knowing where I belonged that the questions stung. People were trying to define something I couldn't even figure out myself. Maybe they hadn't met a Third Culture Kid before and were struggling to figure out which category to place me in. Underneath their questions, they were wondering the question I was trying to avoid: where are you *really* from?

As I went to more startup events and house parties, I tried to accept this whole 'your accent, I just can't place it' conversational routine. But I wrestled with the internal conversation I was starting to have ('your future, I just can't place it'). If I thought about it too much, I started psychologically hyperventilating. I had moved to Wellington because I thought New Zealand was 'home', but now that I was actually here, I felt more lost than ever.

Up until then, I hadn't seen the point of meditating upon my cultural roots - to be a TCK, to be a global nomad, to be 'neither here nor there' – surely this was just a lens through which to view the world; to focus excessively on the lens itself would neglect the point of it in the first place. Yet I had started to question if this multiplicity within me was a label I tagged onto my response about my background or if being a TCK was a crucial part of the compass guiding my major life decisions.

We all have that compass - the part of us that tells us our True North, what's right from wrong, and whether we're on the right path. But right then, I was making dumb decision after dumb decision. I was pushing away the people who cared about me. I hadn't *felt* anything – anger, joy, melancholy – in ages, even though I was supposed to be following my 'passion'. I was growing ashamed of this negative cloud I seemed to carry.

The more I tried to meet new people in Wellington, the more alone I felt. *What* was driving this numbness? I thought about it a lot. At the heart of it, I wanted to live in multiple places at once: Hong Kong with my parents, Auckland with high school friends, Wellington with my business partner, and London with my brother. I wanted to be everywhere and knew that I couldn't be. It was more than picking a city – it was navigating an identity and a culture to belong to. I wanted to be able to read my inner compass again.

As a gentle middle-aged woman with light brown hair opened the door to her room, I grabbed my handbag and walked into her office. The first impression I got of Annette in just the first ten seconds of small talk is that she seemed really kind, soft-spoken and smart. The room had beige walls and smelled faintly of vanilla. I noticed a box of tissues on the coffee table and hoped I wouldn't have to use them.

"So," Annette said gently. "What brings you here today?"

"Um… yeah, I don't know," I said.

Silence.

I cleared my throat. "I just, well, I haven't been feeling like myself lately."

What I didn't say: I felt like I was wandering through a maze with no end in sight. I felt so disconnected from everyone that it was getting harder and harder to see the point of anything. My thoughts had grown increasingly dark. I was finding it more and more difficult to socialise without wine. I didn't feel like myself, but I wasn't sure who that person even was anymore, or whether I even wanted to step back into being her again.

At the same time, whenever I'd catch these negative thoughts, I'd feel ashamed. After all, what did I have to be sad about? I had a loving family and a university degree and had gone to good schools. I was lucky. Things felt grey, but maybe I was just weak.

What might have helped me at the time was data showing that 90 per cent of TCKs feel out of sync with their peers and that those with highly mobile childhoods are more predisposed to depression. Another study showed that those currently living in their passport culture tended to experience significantly more symptoms of depression than those TCKs who had not returned to their passport culture.

"People come to therapy when they're in pain and want the pain to go away," Annette said to me soon after the session had begun.

Psychological pain, I learned that day, is impossible for anyone else to see. You're trapped in a prison of your own making, and only you hold the key to breaking out of it. I had no idea how to talk about what I was feeling because I barely knew what was going on with me internally. I just knew that something was off.

"Why don't you tell me a bit about yourself?" she asked.

I took a deep breath. When I traced back in my memory to where this had begun, I had a feeling that I should probably tell her about Dane. But first, I started talking about Hong Kong.

[2]

COSMOPOLITAN HALLWAYS

*"A global soul is a person who had grown up in many cultures
all at once - and so lived in the cracks between them."*

- PICO IYER

" GREW UP IN HONG KONG." This was what I told
Annette, a phrase I had said hundreds of times. But this
time, what I meant was this: I grew up at an international crossroads, where everyone was from everywhere, and I
felt most at home when I was in that global mesh. I loved school
(Lisa Simpson was my spirit animal), and I took for granted
that I would always be in a global environment. When you're a
kid, you don't have enough experience to have perspective yet.
You just think that whatever surrounds you is what surrounds
everyone else.

In the 1990s Hong Kong that I knew, the city was in a transition period. It was the final decade of colonial rule in the territory and the Handover was on the horizon. What would change
after 1997? We knew the red post boxes would be painted green,
and the last Hong Kong Governor would be replaced by a new
chief executive. It seemed to be at the heart of all the chat everyone's parents had with their friends.

My friends and I would tune out because we had more pressing items on our agenda, like how late we could push out bedtime, who Jonathan Taylor Thomas was dating, and whether *Full House* would be renewed for another season. For me specifically, I was obsessed with how to get my hands on more copies of *The Baby-Sitters Club* and *Sweet Valley Middle School* novels.

Everyone says their childhood was a simpler time. Mine was simple enough that I can still remember exactly how each weekday began.

"Morning, darling!" Mum would wake me up as the red Mickey Mouse clock on my bedroom wall signalled it was time to start the day. There was always an exclamation mark in her voice. As I mumbled and tried to negotiate for five more minutes, I'd hear her say the same to my younger brother in his room.

In the kitchen, at our round white marble table, we would pour milk over our Fruit Loops as cartoons played on *Star World*. My brother would push around his matchbox cars as our *amah* (housekeeper) Neena would nudge him to finish his breakfast before it was too late.

Then we'd grab a lemon tea from the fridge and snacks with Chinese characters on them and shove them into our backpacks. We'd out the front door, saying goodbye to Dad, who was usually thumbing through the *South China Morning Post*. We'd stroll to the top of a steep concrete hill, where the bus would drive down through the leafy canopy overhead around 8 am. The doors would fling open, and our 'bus mother' would sing at us, "*Jo seng!*" (Good morning!). Her name for me was "*Ad-eh-ri Bai-ro*".

As we were in the English-speaking stream of the French International School, we had classes in English but were taught French four times a week. Sometimes we also did PE, Art or Music in French, when our teachers were from the French stream. They said it was to improve our language skills, but I'm pretty sure now that it was just easier for them in their first language.

On our bus, there were kids from both the French and English streams. On the 15-minute drive to school, I'd hear a mixture of mainly English conversations interspersed with '*Ça va?*' and '*Pour quoi?*' I'd share my Discman headphones with Rachel, a Chinese-Canadian who was in the French stream, and had grown up in Toronto. We'd flick through the CD tracks, listening to Avril Lavigne and Hanson. Sometimes one of us would have our black nylon CD folder with us so that we could switch during the ride or lend them to other friends on the bus.

Once we pulled up to the school parking lot at the Jardine's Lookout campus, we'd file off the buses, Jansport bags on our back, towards the rows of royal blue lockers. Language was fluid, and English was only one way of communicating. If you were walking through the hallway and the French kids were sitting up against their lockers, with their legs and backpacks draped in your path, saying '*excuse me*' didn't get you as far as '*excusez-moi*'.

People would flick back and forth between languages – "Omigod, my Mom was like, 'You can't, you just can't!' And finally, I was like, *d'accord*." That global cocktail of cultures was what I always loved about primary school. It felt like living in an international arrivals hall, where you learned about different corners of the world just by being there.

Back then, kids in France would go to school from 8 a.m. to 4 p.m., with a half-day on Saturday replacing classes on Wednesday. In Hong Kong, our school imitated this but changed it so that Wednesday was a half-day, and there was no Saturday school.

Instead, on Saturdays, we'd hang out at Pacific Place mall. We'd meet at noon outside Jumbo Grade, the stationery store, and often see a movie at UA Cinema. I remember, after the movie, calling Mum to pick me up from the payphones by the escalators, which I had to save a curly-edged two-dollar coin to use.

During those mall trips, or any group gatherings, the usual tween drama was about *loyalty*. Whose side were you on? Who did you believe? *She* said *you* said that but did you agree? Or did you take back what you'd said? This was probably the same for tweens all around the world, whether they went to international schools or not.

Surrounded by Chinese faces in the malls, there would sometimes be other groups of expat kids our age. Hong Kong was both a global hub and, among expats, a small town, where everybody had friends at other schools and generally knew everyone else's business. This grapevine would enable rapid-fire background checks on kids from other schools when people started 'dating' - which meant being 'asked out' to a movie at Pacific Place, brainstorming the outfit over the landline throughout the course of the week, *holding his hand*, and then reporting back.

We probably absorbed what 'dating' was from American movies like *She's All That*. Growing up in this environment meant always being aware that your culture was only part of a larger melting pot. Most expat kids I knew had a British or American accent. The TV shows we watched - not on our laptops like now, but on schedules we had to look up in the newspaper - were primarily American. We read *Sugar* from the UK and *Dolly* magazines from Australia. Culture was something to be consumed instead of a homogenous set of automatically accepted values.

Part of life at an international school meant that everyone was, well, international. This meant that planes were like buses. Travel did not mean the same thing to us that it did to our parents when they were our age, which my parents constantly reminded us about. But we had never known anything different: I had flown before I could walk, when my parents took me as a baby to my Mum's hometown in Malaysia to be baptised.

Travelling was just what most people did to stay connected to their extended families and grandparents. Over summer break, some families would go to the beach in Phuket; others would head to London, and mine would go to Malaysia and New Zealand.

Even during term time at school, we treated the world like our classroom. When we were eleven, a few of us in the drama club were selected to attend the International Schools Theatre Association (ISTA) Festival. I still remember the bliss I felt when I discovered I was one of the chosen ones for the ISTA trip, like I had won an Oscar and a Pulitzer all at once. *I don't think anything will ever beat this feeling,* I wrote in my journal.

We flew to Kuala Lumpur for four days of drama workshops with other kids from international schools around South-East Asia. That wasn't the last global trek we would take as classmates.

When we were thirteen, our class went on a two-week trip to France. We walked around Paris with our cameras and notebooks, hearing and practising the same language we'd grown up with in the hallways. We went to the Louvre, took photos outside Notre Dame, learned to sail catamarans around Saint-Jean-Cap-Ferrat, singing the *Baywatch* theme song and laughing hysterically whenever one of us fell into the water.

As I got older, I realised how privileged we all were. When you're a kid surrounded by other families jetting off to Scotland

and Australia like they're different neighbourhoods as opposed to continents, you can't help but see the world as a global village. You feel at home in airports, and you think it's normal, until you realise that it isn't.

This is part of why I felt ashamed to be sitting in a therapist's office. I had been given so much, so what was I there to complain about? How dare I feel anything negative about what was, on the surface, such a fortunate childhood? What was wrong with me?

Yet as my first therapy session continued, I realised that this nomadic childhood was part of the issue. Back then, the school had never mentioned the term TCK. (I imagine it's different now plus these days there's also social media and Google.) I never called myself by that term. I just always saw myself as my friends and classmates did - we were international school students.

Maybe I wasn't even properly christened as a TCK until the first big move.

"When did you leave Hong Kong?" Annette asked.

"Well, we moved to Auckland just before my fourteenth birthday," I told her. As soon as I said the words, I felt like I was back in the moment from almost a decade ago.

[3]

WE'RE NOT MOVING

"Anyone who has lost something they thought was theirs forever finally comes to realise that nothing really belongs to them."

\- PAULO COELHO

THE DAY THE NEWS BROKE, we were sitting around a white linen tablecloth at the Hong Kong Cricket Club, eating dim sum. We had just had *har gow* (shrimp dumplings) and were waiting for the minced pigeon and lettuce course. Even though we'd had these dishes so many times before, something was different. I felt like this news had been building up for weeks; I'd suspected it was coming. I'd heard my parents discussing it when they thought my brother and I were asleep.

I had just turned thirteen and was nattering on about something pointless at the lunch table, mentioning something about "next year at school", and my mother said, "Oh, but we'll be living in Auckland then."

Sorry, what?

My parents had previously mentioned moving to New Zealand, where my Dad was from, but I hadn't realised that it had been *decided* like that. When had this gone from a family hypothetical to a definite decision? When had this gone from 'someday, maybe' to 'next year'? Where was my say in all of this? Shouldn't we take a vote on things like this?

Of course, like anyone who knows they don't hold the upper hand, I refused to accept this news. I had always assumed that this was some pipe dream of my Dad's, that we would move back to his homeland one day. I didn't think we would actually have to follow through with this. Nothing against New Zealand, but Hong Kong was where our family belonged – always had been, always would be.

"We're not moving," I gasped.

"Oh yes, we are," my Dad said.

"Well, I'm not," I retorted.

This must be some weird joke. Except no one was laughing. My brother was too young to really understand what was going on. Meanwhile, I felt like I was melting inside, and everything had just gone from feeling positive and familiar to a very scary unknown.

Looking back now, my parents' approach to the move was like the way most people approach a toddler when they fall: you tell them to brush it off. But I wasn't a toddler. I was a teenager. I was old enough to feel like school was just starting to get to the good part, with boys and parties and adventures with the friends I had grown up with.

I had been in the same class since I was four, and it had always felt like a second family. The thought of leaving all of them was too much for my mind to handle. But the reality was that we were going to be shipping up and across the world, to a country I had always thought of as nice but not really connected to the rest of the world the way that Hong Kong was at its core.

I can see now that when my parents told us that we were moving, they were trying to protect us from pain by ignoring that it could exist. They were also taking a very pragmatic, rational, and logical approach to the whole thing. In Asia, the general level of emotional touchy-feely chat is very different to the Western world. You don't complain when things get tough. You get over it, get on with it, and if you have to cry about it, do it in private.

Without knowing it, that day, I started going through the stages of grief, the first one being denial. I remember thinking: "This can't be happening, this won't be happening." Since I didn't feel like expressing that out loud, I internalised all of it, and somewhere I must have started to believe that if you're sad, you're weak. If you're strong, you look on the positive side of this: the move would be an opportunity for a fresh start.

Yet in that moment at the Cricket Club, I was distraught, and I felt invisible. When your parents tell you that you're moving, they're telling you that the life you know is going to be over. The person you exist as in this city is dying. You're going to lose daily contact with all the friends, teachers, and people who make up your daily life. Sorry! Game over.

I wasn't going to take this lying down. The next day, I booked a meeting with my headmistress to discuss what we could do about this. It was time to mobilise and fight! I passionately tried to convince my headmistress to join my campaign to convince my parents that it would be disastrous to my grades, nay, my entire academic future (!) if we moved there.

She gently told me that she couldn't cooperate. She knew this was tough, but she promised it would eventually get easier.

Fine, then. I wouldn't cooperate either. When my parents took me later that year to see schools in Auckland, I refused to speak to the interviewer at the second school we saw. I kept silent the whole way through, like a silently protesting civil rights activist, until my Mum nudged me. Then I felt guilty and grunted out a few words.

Luckily, my report card (nerd) must have made up for my moodiness. Or the interviewer was used to sullen teenagers. Or maybe they thought it was cute that I was so *mad*. In any case, I ended up getting accepted into the co-ed school in Auckland, which was a relief. Having gone to a co-ed school my entire life up until then, switching to the alternative – an all-girls school – would have been an even bigger nightmare on top of everything else.

I know my parents made the decision out of love for us: they wanted us to experience having 'a national identity' in New Zealand. I know that they broke the news the best way they knew how. But right then, it just seemed unbelievably unfair, and I refused to go along with this injustice without a fight.

It wasn't just the present that I was sad about losing. It was the future I had always imagined for myself. My parents couldn't know this because I don't think I ever mentioned it to them, but I had mapped out a vision of how I thought my teenage years would go in Hong Kong. These two people were meant to have my back, and now they were telling me that this dream life was over before it had even begun.

I had always seen myself writing for The Channel (the high school newspaper) and joining the Hong Kong Players (the theatre group). I had always assumed that I'd get to help edit the yearbook. I had always imagined that the guys I'd date would be from the other international schools in Hong Kong. There had been so many things that I had been looking forward to; a set of experiences that life had been paving towards. Suddenly, without warning, it was all starting to crumble like a landslide.

Nobody else could see how much I was looking forward to spending my high school years in Hong Kong. I did not want to start all over again when making friends in high school because

I had spent my whole life up until then with the same friends. We had gone to primary school together, and done so many trips together, from Cheung Chau island to France. High school was going to be the time when we'd finally get to do all the exciting things we'd watched the grades above us experience.

I sometimes wonder if it would have been easier if I'd been younger or older, and I know that it would have stung at any age. But where do those futures go for TCKs? All the roads we never got to walk down all the way to the end? The people we never got to become, the friendships we never got to develop, the class memories we never got to participate in?

I didn't share *all* of this with Annette. I gave her a rough outline of how much of a shock it had been to realise that we were moving. Even just telling the story, I realised I was secretly harbouring some residual feelings about it all. Having not really felt anything for what seemed like ages, I suddenly felt the flicker of feeling a whole lot.

"That's a tough age to move," she said.

"Yeah, it was," I said.

Thank you, I said inside my head. Wow, this stuff had happened nearly a decade ago. I was still hanging onto it? I hadn't even thought about these things in years, especially recent years when I'd been so busy with yMedia that I regularly forgot to eat.

I didn't know it at the time, but this session would be where I started to remove the thorn in my subconscious that had been troubling me for months, causing a deep and deafening loneliness. I couldn't understand or accept that loneliness because it seemed illogical to be feeling what I was feeling.

Later on, I read a survey showing that if TCKs were asked what characterised them the most, they almost all answered "their ability to shift identities depending on cultural settings."

Like cultural sponges or chameleons, TCKs can learn to adapt to any situation. This characteristic can be a 'curse' as the rapid adaptability to multiple cultures can contribute to "lacking a sense of cultural belonging" and get in the way of identity formation.

That curse had found me. Sigmund Freud used to say that "depression is anger turned inwards", and that session was where I learned to pause and soothe everything bubbling inside me. Immediately I felt like coming to therapy had been the first truly good decision I'd made in ages, even though I still had no idea where it was all going to lead.

[4]

THE NEW GIRL

"Friendship is the hardest thing in the world to explain. It's not something you learn in school. But if you haven't learned the meaning of friendship, you really haven't learned anything."

MUHAMMAD ALI

MY FIRST DAY OF SCHOOL in Auckland was when I realised what it meant to be a TCK – before I knew what the term meant. I had just turned fourteen, recently started wearing contact lenses, and started becoming conscious about emerging red bumps on my forehand, which I dutifully covered with thick layers of Maybelline foundation.

"You're going to have a great day," Mum told me as she and Dad dropped me off. I could tell she was a little nervous for me, but I appreciated it and the fact that she was, as usual, trying to be so positive. I was excited, nervous, dreading this, and curious about how it would all turn out. It was strange wearing a uniform (with a tie!) for the first time in my life and having no idea what to expect in terms of a class schedule.

I showed up for Science class with Mrs Orange, who introduced me to the class ("This is Adele, she's just moved here from Hong Kong, be nice to her"). As I sat down in the first row at the closest empty seat I could see, the first thing I noticed about everyone in my class was their accents. They were so Kiwi. Or I was just so not Kiwi – my accent was pretty much American next to theirs.

I'd never thought that much about accents before – back in Hong Kong at my international school, everyone had a weird accent that was sort of British or Americanised. If you didn't have a weird accent, that was weird. Here, "no" was pronounced "noiiiii" and "I don't know" was "I don't knooiii" and it was funny to be around that.

In Hong Kong, I'd been "the Kiwi one" in my class. Now that I was with Kiwis, I was "the new girl from Hong Kong." You learn that as a TCK, your home zone is the in-between. When you're with locals, you realise that you have to keep parts of yourself invisible. It took a few interactions with my schoolmates before this concept started dawning on me.

Back in Hong Kong, plenty of people had been part of the international school circuit – a friend from my school bus, Dan, was Caucasian but had gone to school in Japan, then Manila, then Hong Kong, then moved to the U.K. Asking someone where they were from had been as natural as asking what their name was.

The real moment when it clicked that I was going to have to slightly edit myself if I was going to fit in around here came when I was walking with a girl called Elena who had a pixie haircut. Like everyone else I'd asked that morning, I asked her, "Where are you from?" And she said, "Auckland," but she said it in such a dismissive, "duh!" way that I started to feel stupid for asking.

Here, *everyone* was from Auckland. Everyone was Kiwi. The question I had always used as a key way to figure someone else out was now totally pointless. Meanwhile, my new classmates couldn't understand why I had an American accent and kept asking me what Japan was like. ("What – isn't Hong Kong in Japan?")

I had stepped behind a glass cage, and though I could be here physically with these people, I was somewhere else emotionally. I stopped asking where people were from. Unless instructed otherwise, I assumed that people were from Auckland.

I couldn't explain myself to these new faces, and they couldn't understand me even if they tried. At fourteen, I don't think I even knew what I was trying to get them to understand. I often daydreamed about walking down Queen's Road Central in Hong Kong, the faces from my old school bus, and how much I missed hearing French in the hallways. Nobody read *Sugar* magazine here.

I missed being in a global kaleidoscope, where everyone was coming and going. In Auckland, everyone was born here and stayed here. It was the first time I recognised the extent to which I'd be trapped within myself, trying to connect with peers, but feeling like we had completely different operating systems.

Later I would learn that this is a common sentiment among TCKs and that many repatriating TCKs feel similar isolation. It's normal as a TCK to have identity issues during repatriation and challenges developing strong social relationships. Instead, there's a perpetual sense of being 'different' when returning to their passport countries as adolescents. The cultural gaps are especially painful when you're a teenager, and all you want to do is fit in.

I was learning all of this through experience but didn't have the language to make sense of it just yet. Years later, I went on to read countless other tales of TCKs who return to their home country to feel exactly what I felt in those early days of school in New Zealand – your passport says you are from this country, so you feel like you should be able to blend right in. Even if you manage to fit in on the surface, there's a part of you that doesn't feel like you truly belong because your memories and points of reference are so different.

To me, being a TCK means wearing a badge that denotes you are global as opposed to local, that you belong everywhere and nowhere, and that you have a mosaic of memories that can be hard to explain to people who have grown up in homogeneous cultures. From a young age, you're also aware that there is no single definition of normality – growing up inside a melting pot shows you that truth is subjective and differences are to be respected.

Being a TCK means having a private view of what it's like to float above your life in different cities as a whole, as opposed to being able to stand fully immersed in one place and declare, 'This is home.' Instead, it becomes, 'This is home (for now).' That's what I kept reminding myself of during those first days of high school.

A real Kiwi didn't have an American accent. Just like a real Malaysian understood Malay. I learned over time that the only *real* thing I was, was an expat kid – someone who felt at home at the intersection of cultures and not at the centre point of any of them. The closer I got to the centre of any given culture, the lonelier I felt.

This was brought to me on my first day of school in Auckland, where I could immediately tell that I didn't fit in. I knew it would be challenging to do so unless I seriously edited myself. It was only a few years, and then I'd be able to go somewhere else for university. Auckland wasn't *home* home. This was just where we were living now. This was just a rest stop. I was going to try and get through as best I could.

Funnily enough, it was during a holiday back in Asia that I finally found some of the answers I needed. My parents had assumed that I was settling into my Auckland school because getting good grades was still important to me (Lisa Simpson style) and I seemed to be making friends. Although there's a massive difference between making friends and making *close* friends, and that took a while longer.

During the Auckland school holidays, my family and I went to Hua Hin, a beachside town in Thailand. I'd packed some books that had looked interesting in Borders, including *The 7 Habits of Highly Effective Teens* by Sean Covey. Modelled on his father's book, which was designed for the aspiring leaders (read: middle managers) of corporate America, the book spoke to me in a way that I really needed at the time.

I remember starting to read it by the pool while my parents napped. Even after just a few chapters, it felt like a hundred light bulbs were going off inside me. Some of the gems included Covey saying: "These problems are real, and you can't turn off real life. So I won't try. Instead, I'll give you a set of tools to help you deal with real life."

As a teenager, you're dealing with a lot, TCK or not. You're self-conscious about getting noticed, but you want more than anything to feel visible. You don't quite have control over your schedule yet, and all you want is to be taken seriously. You're not a kid anymore, but you're not quite in charge of yourself either. In my case, I felt like I'd been snatched from an environment where I could fully be myself and dropped on a foreign planet.

In high school, I often thought about how easy it would be to fall into a world of one. When you're a TCK, you carry the memories of a place that your classmates may not have even heard of. You feel like an alien, but you either use what makes you different to set you apart in a positive or a sad way.

I struggled to adjust to the idea of never moving back to Hong Kong, but I now saw that in those make-or-break moments, I could treat it as a scary path or as an adventure.

That book helped me learn a few habits that, decades later, I still remember. It covered things like 'how to be proactive' and 'how to actively listen'. It talks about the importance of owning your decisions and taking responsibility for the things you can control.

At the time, it also taught me this: *you're not in Hong Kong anymore, and it's time to get over it.* I had to let go of the grief I'd been feeling for *myself*. Not for my parents or anyone else. I didn't want to spend all of my years in Auckland wallowing. I wanted to see the move to this new school as an opportunity (to do exactly what, I hadn't figured out yet), and I wanted to make the most of it instead of seeing myself as a victim.

It was sunset as I lay on a hammock near our hotel room, eagerly soaking up the final pages of the paperback. The sky was turning cotton-candy pink and orange as I closed the book with a smile. Sean Covey got it. He'd given me something I didn't realise I needed. A one-way pep talk I couldn't get from my parents, friends, teachers, brother or anyone else.

I could see now that this move to New Zealand had been unexpected, but it didn't have to be the worst thing that had ever happened. While some things were beyond my control, there were other things I could still influence. I could still have dreams of how I wanted my future to turn out. I could still set goals because they gave me control over my life. I could make the most of all that lay ahead. It would sure beat staring at old photos of my Hong Kong classmates and trying not to cry.

[5]

SCHEMAS

"We repeat what we don't repair."

MARY BETH KEANE

COULDN'T FIND THE WORDS TO get all of this out during the first therapy session. I didn't tell Annette about Mrs Orange or Pacific Place or the Sean Covey book. At that point, I was still trying to figure out what had led me to book a therapy appointment in the first place. Then she hit on the question that I knew would open another library of issues.

"Are you dating anybody at the moment?" Annette asked.

I'd always just been friends with guys. I'd had close friends who happened to be male, from primary school to high school to university. From secondary school, sure, sometimes we'd kiss, and we would become 'crushes' for a season. But from high school onwards, something in me would freeze whenever anything got too close or deep. I chalked it up to the Lois Lane scene I'd watched when I was nine years old, which resonated with me even back then.

In the pilot of *Lois & Clark* with Teri Hatcher and Dean Cain, there's a scene where Lois comes home from work, and her sister is pressuring her about 'getting out there' and 'meeting men'. Lois talks about how she's just not interested in those men, how much of a waste of time it seems, and then she goes to her room and watches television while she's in bed eating popcorn. A black-and-white love scene flickers onto her TV screen, and she starts crying while eating popcorn. Even as I watched that as a kid, something felt familiar. Choosing work over love because it's easier. Avoiding vulnerability. As a kid, I didn't have the framework for it, but the scene always stuck.

The way this played out when I was a teenager: I would always invest way more time, energy, interest and love into my female friendships than in anything romantic with the opposite sex. Even when there was a crush or potential romance, I'd automatically dismiss it. By the time I was 21 and at university, I was starting to think that my mode of operation when it came to guys had to change or I would be alone forever. There had been a string of pseudo-relationships, but they had never converted into anything serious, and lately, one particular memory had lingered.

"Well, there was this guy earlier this year," I said to Annette. "I still don't really get what happened."

I'd met Dane at the start of the year back at university in Melbourne. He was a British exchange student with dark blonde hair and blue eyes in one of my classes who vacillated between class clown and teacher's pet – often asking questions, giving his opinion, and raising his hand. He was like this with everyone outside of class, too – whenever we made small talk in the hallways, he seemed genuinely interested in whatever anyone was talking about.

Somehow during one of those chats, it came up that he had briefly lived in Malaysia and that my Mum was from there; then we started talking on Facebook and went to a Thai restaurant for our first date. Soon that turned into hanging out a couple of times a week, watching *Peep Show* on the couch, and walking to class together. As long as we were in friendship territory with some kissing and cuddling, I was fine, and enjoyed hanging out and getting to know him. Dane's mother had passed away recently, and he'd talk to me about her late at night. I felt special to be the one he told those things to, but it also felt unfamiliar as I'd never gotten this close to any guy.

One Sunday morning, about six weeks after we'd started hanging out, Dane and I stood in the kitchen making pancakes. As he pulled me closer to kiss him, the batter started sizzling, and I started giggling and gesturing towards the pan. He broke away for a second, flipped the pancake over, put his arms around my waist and leaned back toward me. Right then, something in me lurched. This was different.

We could talk for hours. He made me laugh, and he laughed at my dumb jokes. We could play together and have fun, but I could also tell him my secrets. I cared about his opinion, I admired how his brain worked, and we were both interested in having adventures: we wanted to see the world, write, and work in digital media. This was the closest I'd ever been to a great relationship.

He was the first guy I'd felt this way about. I wanted to bring him back to Hong Kong to meet my family. I wanted to introduce him to my high school friends from Auckland. I wanted to go over to England and meet *his* friends and family. The 'normal' reaction to all of this should be joy. I knew that, and part of me felt really, really happy just at the thought of little notes Dane had left me and dates we had planned. Then when Dane brought up the 'what-are-we' chat on the phone one day, my Lois-Lane tendencies reared their ugly head.

Did I really want a *relationship*? Well, maybe it wasn't the right time for anything too serious. I was moving back to New Zealand soon to work on yMedia. But did I want Dane? Yes. So then – why wasn't I trying to make him my boyfriend? I didn't even understand it myself, so I tried to avoid it and came up with some non-answer that pushed the conversation into 'undefined' territory.

Soon afterwards, Dane and I were on our way to class one morning, and he power-walked on ahead of me so that he could get into class earlier. We'd agreed he'd do that because we didn't want to tell everyone else we were dating. His walking ahead of me then caused a minor panic attack and made me feel like the walls were caving in. I called Pam, who was in New Zealand, to tell her how confused I was. I was falling for this guy, and I didn't want to end it, but I didn't want to start anything serious that could derail our plans for moving to Wellington and working on yMedia. What should I do and how could I not hurt him, and what even was this?

She tried her best to understand why I was getting so anxious about Dane being amazing. ("Surely that's a *good* thing, isn't it?") I tried to explain that yMedia was one of the most exciting things I had ever worked on, and I wanted to give it *everything*. That meant not getting distracted, no matter how wonderful this guy seemed. At least, that's how I rationalised it.

The thing about anxiety is that it's rarely rational. It's our body's internal alarm system, its way of screaming DANGER even when there is no actual hazard.

Later that week, I called Dane and told him we shouldn't keep seeing each other. In my head, I kept insisting, *please don't buy this! I don't mean it!* Out loud, I talked about moving back to New Zealand after graduation and not wanting to let this get too serious in case we ended up getting hurt. After we hung up, I cried. But I felt like I'd done the right thing, like I'd protected both of us from something terrible.

The next day, we saw each other in class. I texted him, inviting him to a sushi lunch with a group of us from class afterwards. He said no. *Wait, was he mad?* Didn't he know I'd pushed him away *because* I liked him? Didn't he know that deep down,

I did really want to be with him – I just had other obligations, another person to be, somewhere else, and being here with him was just going to interfere with that?

The regret lingered around me like a bad smell I kept trying to wash off but couldn't. As immune as I'd been to depending on guys, I wasn't immune to this one, and I'd royally messed it all up and had nobody to blame but myself. The closer Dane got, the more anxious I became. I thought I had come to therapy because I didn't know where to settle down, but maybe I had come here because no matter where I was, I was struggling to let myself get attached to anyone.

Why was that? This wasn't who I wanted to be. This person who had run away from a guy who could have become something, perpetually searching for someone that didn't exist, and always wanting to escape from what they claimed they wanted.

"Let me show you something," Annette said, pulling out a blue folder from her desk drawer. She pierced a hole into my grey thoughts and let some light in by taking out an A4 sheet of paper with *Maladaptive Schemas* printed across the top.

"Have you ever heard of this?"

I shook my head.

"A schema is how we see the world," she said. "They are perceptions we build up over time and reinforce through experience. The more experiences we have reinforcing those schemas, the stronger they become."

A maladaptive schema, she explained, was a toxic or unhealthy way of seeing the world. It refers to a self-defeating or dysfunctional theme, first experienced during childhood or adolescence. These themes get strengthened throughout a lifetime, often leading to negative beliefs. Everyone experienced them to some extent, she explained. Some schemas were just stronger than others. By being aware of our schemas, we could begin healing those causing us pain.

Science. Data. Psychology. There was an explanation of why things felt so out of whack. Seeing this piece of paper with black-and-white terminology was the most liberating feeling I'd experienced since that kiss with Dane in the kitchen. Something about all of this gave me hope that I wouldn't feel hollow forever.

"Now, I want to give you some exercises before your next session," Annette said. Homework? My kind of party. "I'd like you to complete a few questions on a handout I'll give you. And, if you have time, I'd like you to read this."

If I had time? I'd been waiting for an extra-credit assignment for years. She gave me a copy of a yellow and red book with the title *Reinventing Your Life* splashed across the cover. Maybe this book would do for me in Wellington what Sean Covey had done for me in Hua Hin.

I wanted to reinvent things if it meant I could feel like myself again. I was starting to see that no matter which city I chose to live in and how many times I moved, the same things would follow me until I looked inwards and started facing them.

[6]

AMBIGUOUS LOSS

"And everything dies, baby, that's a fact. But maybe everything that dies someday comes back."

BRUCE SPRINGSTEEN

A SINGLE THERAPY SESSION DIDN'T FIX everything, even though I left that first session feeling like a huge weight had been lifted. So I wasn't nuts. According to Annette, I was depressed, and contrary to what I'd thought, it didn't mean being sad. It meant feeling numb. But she made me realise that this was a hard chapter, but it was part of a longer story.

The more I started to explore everything around maladaptive schemas with Annette, the more I began to see that there had been another element to my TCK childhood and teenage years. It was like I'd been watching the same movie for years without realising that there was a hidden soundtrack.

On the surface, everything had been great. Case in point: a joint farewell-and-birthday party in Hong Kong with my friend Camilla when we were about to turn fourteen. We'd invited our class to celebrate at the Hong Kong Cricket Club, and I remember thinking we were *so* cool with our plastic metallic chokers as we danced around the function room in skirts from Marks & Spencer and spaghetti strap tops.

That night, *Pure Shores* from *The Beach* soundtrack played, followed by All Saints, and we warbled the words to Lady Marmalade – *"Voulez-vous couchez avec moi?"* Around the wooden dance floor, we giggled and wiggled our eyebrows at each other - since we all spoke French, we knew exactly what those words translated into.

We had the innocence that came with the pre-digital era, where we all used dial-up modems. We played Minesweeper. We had chickmail email addresses. We had just started speaking on ICQ instant messaging. As for real-life messages, we used to carry notebooks where we would write notes to one another in rainbow-coloured gel pens.

I still remember the cheesy quote that I scribbled in far too many of them during the yearbook-signing season: "Don't cry because it's over, smile because it happened." This wasn't just something that I wrote carelessly. This was something I held onto tightly as a core life philosophy.

I had always thought it was a positive sentiment. But therapy was now helping me see that it could also be a form of emotional denial. If you don't let yourself get sad sometimes, you slowly become a robot with a smile painted on its face.

Maybe I had already started learning this through the goodbyes over the years. Two years before that Cricket Club bash, there had been another joint birthday party, this time with my friend Jess. It was a June night, and it was at her place in Chung Hom Kok, a beachside suburb in the southern part of Hong Kong Island.

The party was on the ground floor, an open-air basement with an island-shaped pool and lawn, surrounded by a border of tall palm trees. We had soft gooey chocolate cake, and every-one sang *Happy Birthday*, after which our classmate Michael fell into the pool with his clothes on.

Then *Truly Madly Deeply* by Savage Garden started playing on the boombox, and as the lyrics drifted through, I started slow-dancing with Dan, a gangly six-feet-tall friend from the school bus. He was moving away to England that summer.

We gingerly glued our bodies together and orchestrated a joint gentle sway to the music. As I rested my head against his chest, I felt sad, but I also knew this was life at an international school. There was a never-ending baggage claim of kids whose parents were pilots or worked for corporations, and 'Dad's job' was usually the reason we often had to say goodbye.

There were farewell parties each year. The person left. Life went on. You had to roll with it. You didn't talk about it. You didn't acknowledge it. You just dealt with it. By the time I was eleven, I had gotten used to these annual goodbyes. But there was something about saying goodbye to Dan that felt different. The school bus had bookended each day: you start and end the day with those friends. Now, he was going.

It was this aspect of being a Third Culture Kid that I always found hard to deal with – the way your lives can intertwine with another and then be permanently disconnected by greater forces.

That night at the party, I realised that I could choose to become like Teflon – interacting with people based on a shell I'd constructed. Or, I could take the risk, get close, and face the sting when the separation comes.

Sometimes there wasn't even a farewell party. The first time a goodbye had stung was when my friend Lizzie moved away at nine years old. When we drove to her house one evening for our final play date, I asked Mum what it all meant in the car.

"It means she's going to school somewhere else, in another country, but you'll always be friends," Mum explained as she put on her indicator and peered over the dashboard.

But how could we still be friends if I never saw her? I didn't understand.

Mum tried to spell it out for me, but it didn't make much sense.

Now that I had started therapy, I was learning about 'ambiguous loss' - which refers to unfinished business without closure or understanding. Ambiguous loss is more subtle and invisible. It differs from the more 'obvious' forms of loss, like death when you're 'allowed' to grieve.

It was coined in the 1970s by educator and researcher Dr Pauline Boss. After working in family therapy, she used it to describe the unresolved loss of families, like those mourning a soldier missing in war. The scope of definition for ambiguous loss has since broadened and can explain what many TCKs experience.

Ambiguous loss happens without a likely chance of achieving emotional closure or a clear understanding. It describes 'leaving without goodbye or 'goodbye without leaving.' Since it often refers to a subtle disappearance, it is harder to recognise and acknowledge. According to Boss, "The greater the ambiguity surrounding one's loss, the more difficult it is to master [the loss] and the greater one's depression and anxiety."

It is difficult for a person to resolve grief if they don't know if the loss is temporary or final. There is a lack of a clear, symbolic ritual surrounding the loss – unlike an actual death, there is no funeral or opportunity to recognise or acknowledge the loss.

This lack of recognition and acknowledgement can lead to a sense of disenfranchisement. Since the losses are invisible, the grief related to these losses is likely to be disenfranchised - as in, ignored or minimised.

Ambiguous loss, and the unresolved grief that comes with it, is a crucial element of the TCK experience. I knew from my own experiences that as a TCK, a world you used to know becomes shut off to you whenever you move. It fades from your access, and everything you loved and lost in the transition remains visible to you and you alone.

Saying goodbye to friends each year had been hard but saying goodbye to them all at once when we moved to New Zealand was a whole other level of loss. My friends weren't the only ones I missed after moving to Auckland. It was the security guards at our apartment, our swim coach – the people I couldn't stay in touch with because our connection was based on logistics.

During high school in Auckland, I missed our *amah* Neena. I missed the drama buddies who had been in the class above mine, and the bus mother. I missed the 15-minute drive through the trees from home to school. These felt like silly things to mourn, so instead, I dismissed them.

But therapy was teaching me to recognise these more complex brands of losses.

In between sessions with Annette, I started to put some of the puzzle pieces together. I guessed that not all TCKs had Lois Lane tendencies. Not all TCKs struggled with the anxiety I had felt when Dane and I started growing close. But I knew that most TCKs struggled with belonging. Perhaps those goodbyes and subtle losses over the years had done something to my psyche that I was finally beginning to recognise.

When we don't experience grief, it freezes, preventing closure – instead, we feel something is perpetually missing. As researcher Kathleen Gilbert put it, without acknowledging the losses and parting 'appropriately', this grief can lurk beneath the surface. In her paper *Loss and Grief between and Among Cultures: The Experience of Third Culture Kids*, she explores how TCK grief may go undiscovered for many reasons. Children manifest grief differently than adults, so adults might miss the signs of it, treat it as banal, and try to emphasise the positive aspects of transition without adequately addressing the loss.

There were many minor heartbreaks that I had glossed over at the time, thinking that skipping over pain made me more responsible. Whether it was saying goodbye to Lizzie or Dan, I had learned that if you stay independent, losses hurt less. The more of a wall you built up, the less others could hurt you through leaving. You say enough goodbyes as a kid, and you can get scared of ever letting anybody in too deep. You move countries enough times and get so good at fitting in that sometimes you forget how to get attached.

Yet now, after what had happened (or failed to happen) with Dane, I realised that refusing to feel emotion doesn't mean you are strong. It means you're in denial. The Sufi poet Rumi said, "You have to keep breaking your heart until it opens." Even though I hadn't spoken to him in months out of sheer embarrassment for how I had behaved, it turns out that an almost-love story had been the heartbreak that started to unlock mine.

After a couple of sessions with Annette, I randomly felt the urge to send Dane a message. It was late on a weeknight, and I was the last one left at the co-working space. I was flicking through others' holiday pictures on Facebook and then started to draft a message. How do you apologise for being such a jerk? I typed out a long message, rewrote it five times, then deleted it. Sometimes, there is nothing left to say.

[7]

IRON HEART

*"In the same way that a claustrophobic will not enter
a room unless he knows there are readily accessible
windows and doors, a commitment phobic will not enter a
relationship unless he knows he can find a way out."*
STEVEN CARTER

DURING THOSE FIRST SESSIONS WITH Annette, I kept thinking back to Dane. I knew that he would have moved on with someone else by now, and deep down, I didn't think we were meant to be together. It wasn't *him* that I felt hung up on but instead the way I had behaved towards him. I was ashamed of the way I had communicated, and I was still stumped as to why I had been so cold. Was it social anxiety? I hadn't labelled it, but maybe that's what it was.

Instead, I had seen it as a feeling of dread interlaced with joy every time he did or said something sweet. I had played a weird mental game where for each daydream about him, I would match it up to a reason why we could never 'really' be together.

When I first met Dane, I loved that he wanted to become a journalist. But now, I found myself questioning – were we too similar? When we first met, I loved that he had travelled. Now I found myself thinking that we would travel too much if we did end up together. Never mind that we hadn't even said "I love you" – suddenly, I would find legitimate reasons for obliterating the idea that we could ever become a couple.

Reading *Reinventing Your Life* reminded me how much books and stories could provide answers to things that were too hard to talk about with others. Much like Sean Covey had inspired me in Hua Hin with his *7 Habits*, Janet S. Klosko and Jeffrey Young offered examples of how maladaptive schemas could be understood and overcome. These books were like passports into other worlds, helping me to learn how things could be different and better.

The schema that I spent a lot of time reading about was abandonment, which according to them, was the primary reason why we experience anxiety in relationships. They talked about how some people preferred to skip relationships altogether or sabotage them early on due to the overwhelming stress generated through emotional intimacy. The diagnostic questionnaire included statements like 'people have always come and gone in my life' and 'in the end, I will be alone'.

Besides reading about the maladaptive schemas, I went deeper down the rabbit hole. Maladaptive schemas had been the gateway drug, and now I wanted the stronger stuff. I moved onto reading about commitment phobia: the resistance or aversion to making decisions around long-term goals.

Previously I had associated the term with emotionally unavailable movie characters who left their fiancées at the altar. The more I read about what the phobia actually entailed, the more I began to recognise familiar patterns in the stories. I found myself ordering a pile of books – *Men Who Can't Love* and *He's Scared, She's Scared* and a bunch of others that I might have been slightly embarrassed to pick up at a physical bookstore.

The more I read, the more I recognised myself. While the books seemed a bit dated at times, referring to the 'male' dynamic of pulling away from a relationship 'once it got too serious', I realised soon enough that I had been behaving like the Man Who Can't Love. I hated recognising some of my behaviours in the protagonists of these psychology books, but I couldn't ignore the parallels between the case studies given and certain episodes in my own life.

Commitment phobics might think and say they want togetherness because somewhere inside themselves, they do. They yearn for the positive aspects of companionship, for the joys that come from being in a relationship and sharing your life with another person.

However, the idea of actually having to tie themselves down to anyone else leaves commitment phobics feeling inexplicably trapped. So while a commitment phobic may talk about the partner they hope to find someday, when they meet a potential partner, their phobia will sabotage the relationship from transcending into reality.

It's a lot like claustrophobia, an irrational fear of confined spaces. There is the irrational sense that you cannot exit if you form any kind of deep attachment to another person. The anxiety is similar to the one a person might feel with claustrophobia – the sensation of feeling suffocated.

The warped reasoning in a commitment phobic's head is that the nicer somebody is to you, the more they are trying to tie you down and emotionally suffocate you. I remembered this from the way I felt the day after Dane made us those pancakes. Although Dane and I had only been seeing each other for a brief time, I felt like the kinder he was to me, the more he was trying to 'trap' me. (Not just, you know, getting to know me.) I felt like continuing to see him would imply that we were destined for a permanent relationship. (Not like, we would never have to build a relationship unless it suited both of us, at a pace other than what suited both of us.)

Most phobias are our minds playing tricks on us. The worst lies are those we don't realise we're telling ourselves. To counteract the fear of being locked down, the mind starts to pick apart another person it once found attractive. In this way, it disqualifies the other person as a potential partner and frees the commitment-phobic from feelings of guilt and confusion and anxiety.

It is an entirely illogical paradox: the better the chemistry, the scarier the possibility of becoming 'tied down' and the more imperative it becomes to escape from the other person. The deeper you click with a person, the more you want to distance yourself. The more fun you have, the more your brain starts coming up with reasons why you can't be together, why this person is wrong for you, and why this will never work.

It can lead to developing an iron heart. Nothing gets in, and so nothing can hurt you. But wearing that coat of steel makes you immune to all the joys that can come with closeness too.

I had realised that the way I was with romantic partners was the way I was with cities too. (Commitment phobia often applies to areas in life beyond romantic relationships.) I had been hopping from Auckland to Melbourne to Wellington as if the plane were a bus. This was a game I played thinking that I was keeping myself 'safe', but in reality, I was just keeping myself at a distance.

Through reading about commitment phobia, I saw that the patterns seemed to align with TCK traits. Commitment phobics felt claustrophobic if anyone got too close, and freedom was part of their psychological DNA. Similarly, TKCs were often defined as rootless and restless.

In fact, TCKs were described by Dr. Ruth Hill Useem as having a prolonged or delayed adolescence. In an article she co-wrote with Ann Baker Cottrell, they mention that in a survey of nearly 700 adult TCKs, ranging from age 25 to 80, only one out of every 10 said that they felt completely attuned to everyday life. The other 90 percent reported that they felt more or less "out of synch" with their age group throughout their lifetimes:

> "Being out of step with those around them is especially noticeable (and painful) in the late teens and twenties when choice of mate, occupation, and lifestyle are being worked out. Some young adult TCKs strike their close peers, parents, and counsellors as being self-centred adolescents, as not being able to make up their minds about what they want to do with their lives, where they want to live, and whether or not they want to 'settle down, get married, and have children.' They have what some call 'prolonged adolescence.'"

In many ways this aligned with what I was reading about commitment phobia. Something about the unwillingness to commit mirrored a refusal to grow up: constantly exploring options, perpetually wandering down corridors and opening doors but refusing to step through them.

However, there's a difference between being a TCK navigating multiple cultural ties, and developing a phobia that keeps you emotionally isolated. I had never considered commitment phobia because I had always thought that commitment (with the right person) was what I wanted. How could I be scared of something I said I wanted?

"Look inside yourself and your past" was the message that most of the books preached. So with Annette's help and a journal by my bed, I kept looking. I didn't name every single loss from the past decade: the moves, the people I'd said goodbye to along the way. But I began to see how it hadn't all been as simple as I'd once liked to believe.

Sometimes moves need to happen for reasons beyond our control. But there are other times when we keep ourselves in motion so that we don't have to face the things we can't escape. I couldn't put a label on the underlying grief I'd denied over recent years, but something about the sessions with Annette was helping me tap into a fear I hadn't realised was lodged deep inside me.

By taking time to pause inside therapy, I had the chance to look at my life and what I was building and poke holes at habits that were no longer serving me. I saw that the constant moves had been something I almost did out of expectation: there's something better, somewhere else, and this place is just a rest stop because there's another place I need to be.

I saw patterns I'd developed as a coping mechanism. In *Narratives of Third Culture Kids: Commitment and Reticence in Social Relationships*, the authors talk about how TCKs by definition have experiences living among different worlds and how this could be isolating when it comes to social interaction and building long-term friendships. The study looks at how constant moves can make it hard to feel connected, and can expose TCKs to "reticence in social interactions, insecurities and a fear of abandonment" which can lead to commitment issues and intimacy struggles in later life.

The patterns I had developed when I was younger were no longer serving me. I didn't want to fear commitment so much that I stopped myself from getting attached to others. As TCKs, we're hardwired for change. But if we're constantly channel-surfing when it comes to the sets of our own lives, we don't leave room to settle. I didn't want to be so hyper-independent that I ended up alone.

While I knew I might not stay in Wellington for the rest of my life, I didn't want to stop myself from getting close to people. I wanted connection. I wanted to learn how to commit. I wanted to learn how to let people in.

As Pam had pointed out a month after I stopped seeing Dane, "You didn't have to completely end it. You could have just started something, and you could have just seen where it went. He could have visited here, you could have visited him – you took the flights when you had to make it work for work, so why not make it work when it comes to a guy?"

She was right, but it was too late by then. This demon had always lurked inside me, invisible to anyone except those who got too close. Maybe some fears always find you, no matter how far you run. Taking time to pause during therapy helped me see a way through the barriers I had created. I didn't know it then, but I was on the verge of one of my biggest breakthroughs in that exact arena.

[8]

TUESDAY NIGHT LOVE

"This morning, with her, having coffee."
JOHNNY CASH
(when asked his definition of paradise)

AFTER ALMOST A MONTH OF twice-weekly sessions with Annette, I felt more like myself and like the colour was coming back into my personality. I started to feel again and had opinions on *The Notebook* (sappy but sweet), sweet potato fries (the best ones were at Sweet Mother's Kitchen), and how to spend a solo weekend afternoon (browsing Unity Books). Soon enough, I started to feel more excited about living in Wellington and saw all these things about the city that I had previously been too numb to notice.

One of the best things was how walkable it was, especially compared to Auckland, where you needed a car and half an hour to get anywhere. In Wellington, our co-working space was a ten-minute walk to my flat, which was a ten-minute walk from Pam's house. We could arrange a group dinner *that afternoon* for later that evening, at KK Malaysian or Chow or one of the other many restaurants, as most people could just walk there.

There were also so many beautiful beaches. From some angles, Wellington's southern coast looks like Hawaii, with its mountains rising majestically from the oceans. After work or during lunchtime in the summer, people from our co-working space would often take a short walk and go swimming in the harbour. On weekends, Pam and I would sometimes borrow a car and drive out to Lyall's Bay or Island Bay. One of our favourite brunch spots was at Maranui cafe, on the top floor of a Surf Life Saving Club.

There was more of a tech community than any other city I'd experienced, with more software than property developers, more tech investors than bankers, and more startups than multinationals. Any community is just a series of overlapping social circles, and most circles we came across in Wellington were friendly, generous, and unpretentious.

Pam and I were getting to know all kinds of different groups, thanks to our co-working space and the nature of yMedia. Like many twentysomething startup founders, we often seemed semi-permanently in business development mode. As I started warming to Wellington, new doors started opening.

I asked friends who had friends in the city to set me up on outings with women they thought I'd get along with and started going on a series of blind dates for friendship. This is how I met Sue. Our first date was at a cocktail bar in the city centre called Concrete, and our connection was instant. It's funny how just one new close friend can make an entire city feel more welcoming.

I was also learning that there was a strength in softness and that iron heart tendencies could be rewired. As C.S. Lewis said, "Love anything and your heart will be wrung and possibly broken. If you want to make sure of keeping it intact you must give it to no one, not even an animal. Wrap it carefully round with hobbies and little luxuries; avoid all entanglements. Lock it up safe in the casket or coffin of your selfishness. But in that casket, safe, dark, motionless, airless, it will change. It will not be broken; it will become unbreakable, impenetrable, irredeemable. To love is to be vulnerable."

I found myself opening up more and letting myself emotionally invest in the city and the people I was meeting. I said yes to more parties and made more effort with new faces I was meeting through work and mutual friends. I stopped worrying about whether Wellington would be a forever place of residence and instead tried to go with the flow more.

For Halloween, Pam's housemates were throwing a party. She and I hadn't bothered to dress up: I wore a Scream mask that had been lying around the office, and she wore some fairy wings. As soon as we walked through her front door, I saw my housemates standing towards the back of the hallway, and I went over to say hi to them and one of their friends, Chase.

I'd met Chase a couple of times before and knew that coincidentally he was an accountant at the same firm as my uncle, that he played rugby, that he had gone to school with my housemates. Their high school stories were often replayed around the flat, all of which had a lot of inside jokes and tales about throwing fruit at each other.

That night, they wore high-necked plaid jumpers and corduroy pants. "We've come as nerds," Chase smirked when I asked him what their costumes were meant to be. I giggled. I had been nursing a bottle of Sauvignon Blanc that night, sipping straight from the brown bag it came wrapped in since the house had run out of glasses and mugs.

Hours flashed by, but I remained glued to the same spot, laughing and touching his elbow a lot. We left the party and started walking downtown, clasping each other's fingers and strolling down the darkened streets hand-in-hand in a quasi-couple way, which felt neither entirely honest nor dishonest, although we were still loosely strangers at that point.

We ended up at a bar that played Bryan Adams' "Summer of 69" and "C'est la vie" by B*Witched. *"Say you will, say you won't, say you'll do what I don't, say you're true, say to me...'"* After a lot of lip-synching, hand-clapping, sipping and giggling, I knew that I'd see him again, and this time, I wouldn't make the same mistakes I had made with Dane. The sessions with Annette had helped a lot. Then again, perhaps different people just bring out different sides of you.

After a few months with Chase, I didn't feel jittery. I felt safe. Over the following months, I discovered that real love is what it sounds like. It's not airbrushed; nobody gallops or loudly declares their affection; there is no soundtrack or beaming moment. The death of the honeymoon period is when the real relationship begins. I realised that growing up was just showing up and wanting to be there again and again.

The moments when I felt the most love were completely non-descript. Lying in still silence, cooking dinner, driving through the Wairarapa region on a Sunday afternoon – these are the things you miss in their absence, the pixels that make up the bigger picture. They're only visible after repeated interaction, but the symphony of the mundane - the shared routines, the shorthand of intimacy – these were everything.

What I learned through Chase is that it takes time to build depth with someone. Before meeting him, I had thought I would only let myself fall for a guy if I was 100 per cent certain that he was The One. But I was learning with Chase that you never found The One – you just met someone you got along with well enough, and eventually, they could become The One.

Chase and I had been dating for almost a year when I got my wisdom teeth removed. That Tuesday afternoon, I left work early, wandered down the road to the dentist, hopped in the leather chair, and listened to the dental nurse instructing me just to relax as she injected me. Everything was a little fuzzy when I started to awake from the anaesthetic, but Chase's familiar frame entered the doorway as I began to see again. He lifted me out of the chair and propped me up as he led me down to the car, where his mother was waiting for us.

I was used to the drive back to his parents' place – they lived a fifteen-minute drive from the city centre, where both Chase and I worked. He had moved back home for six months to save money; he was also doing his accounting exams that year and thought it would be easier for him to focus.

Usually, that drive was a chance to chat about our days or talk about whatever else was on our minds. That day, I passed out. Soon enough, I was back in the room I stayed in at their place, propped up with pillows, with him feeding me yoghurt from a teaspoon because that's all I was allowed to eat. I dribbled a lot, the yoghurt running down my chin, both of us laughing at how attractive I must have looked with saliva-stained chipmunk cheeks and chin.

That episode juxtaposed Friday night love and Tuesday night love, erotic love and companionate love, eros and agape, whatever you want to call it. Weekend nights are when you get the sexiest version of a person; everyone's dressed up with eyeliner on, you're all tipsy, the music's loud and everything and everyone is inherently interesting. I met Chase on a Friday. This guy who now wiped the drool off my face was a different guy from the one I had met that night. I was a different girl from the one he had met; now, he knew my flaws, weak spots, and demons.

While the version of the person you start a relationship with is often different from the person you end up in the relationship with, it takes time before you can tell the difference. It takes time to build up to something that can be lost – there are hundreds of easy replacements for Friday-night infatuation, but Tuesday-night partnership is an entirely different category, with far fewer suitors.

His parents treated me like a daughter, and their house felt familiar in the way that a family home does. There was history in this house; the kids in the family had grown up here. I felt privileged to be part of his family's rituals. As things got more serious with Chase, we often talked about the future, assuming that we'd always be together. Years later, we turned out to be wrong, but we'll always have whatever we were in Wellington. I always think of him on his birthday, and sometimes I wonder how long that will last.

[9]

CHOOSING OUR HERITAGE

*"For we know that our patchwork heritage
is a strength, not a weakness."*

BARACK OBAMA

WHEN DECIDING WHERE TO GO after university, I had chosen Wellington because it seemed like the best place to keep growing yMedia. After several months of seeing Annette, I realised that the initial anchorless ache I'd felt was less to do with the city and more around TCK baggage. As I talked it out in therapy, I eased more into the rhythm of Wellington.

Yet as soon as I started to feel comfortable, another part of me wondered: am I really settling down here, or am I hiding? If I was going to feel this sense of initial discomfort in any city I moved to, was this the city where I wanted to put down roots?

This became especially clear when Obama won the 2008 election. It was in the late afternoon New Zealand time, and I remember being in the co-working space, amazed that everyone was behaving as if it was just a regular day.

This was not a regular day. The world's most famous TCK was about to change the landscape of American politics forever.

"Guys?" I looked at the twenty- and thirty-somethings at the desks around me, but hardly anyone seemed to be talking about what was going on in America. An older guy in the corner was scrolling through news websites, but I'd never talked to him before. Everyone was just doing their work, clicking away on their Macbooks.

Was nobody that interested in global politics? Or maybe I was the weird one, for caring this much about an election in a country that wasn't mine? Everyone was glued to their screens, focused on the code, project, or call summoning them.

This was history in the making and nobody seemed to care! It was as baffling as it was infuriating. Meanwhile, I kept refreshing *The New York Times* every two seconds and texting each one of the new friends I'd made in Wellington to see if anyone wanted to go to a bar (or park, or beach, or restaurant, or anywhere) to celebrate the fact that OBAMA HAD JUST WON OHIO!

My friend Libby, whose older brother I had gone to university with in Melbourne, was the only person I could find who was as exhilarated as I was. We went to celebrate in a nearby Irish bar because it was the only one we could find that was screening the election.

Standing in that bar, thinking about how unaffected everyone had been by such a significant international event, made me remember why I'd been keen to get out of New Zealand after high school. In many ways, the country is ensconced from the rest of the world. This is one of the most attractive things about it. Yet sometimes, the very thing that draws you to a place or a person is the exact thing that ends up frustrating you.

For the rest of my twenties, I wanted to be exploring new parts of the world and discovering, building, creating. Where, though? I still had no idea. Which, on some level, frustrated me, but on another level, I had come to accept. My sessions with

Annette had shown me that some questions don't have simple answers.

I had seen that not everything can be attributed to a schema or a book or a label. Some feelings can't be articulated. Sometimes things happen for no apparent reason. Sometimes life's biggest questions ('where is home?') did not come with one-word answers. Therapy was teaching me to get more comfortable in the grey areas instead of always trying to solve my way out of anything uncomfortable. But what I had never gotten around to discussing in therapy was the question that is the cornerstone of any TCK's experience.

'Where are you from' refers to heritage. Which ancestors created you? From whom did you learn your viewpoints through which you experience the universe? Which nation or belief system are you representing in how you approach the world?

My passport said *New Zealand*; my accent said *an international school*; my memories said *Asia*. No matter how many therapy sessions I went to, some things could not be changed: I had grown up globally and even though I had moved to Wellington trying to trade that in for a more recognisable Kiwi identity, it hadn't been as seamless as I had expected.

For as long as I could remember, I've felt that no matter what city I was in, half of my heart was elsewhere. It had always been that way since I was a kid, and this was either a blessing or a curse depending on how I viewed it. I knew that to commit somewhere was to build a life, but I kept avoiding commitment because to create something meant that it could be taken away at some point.

Besides moving to Auckland at fourteen, my parents took my brother and me to their countries at least once a year while we were growing up – we had always known that the one true 'home' was our little family of four. Home had always been Mum and Dad and my brother – as for culture, we had our own zone of belonging in a triangle between Malaysia, New Zealand, and Hong Kong.

As a result, the choice of knowing where to live had never been simple. I had always wanted to attend university in Melbourne because it was a mid-point between my two frames of reference – Asia and New Zealand. But after four years at the University of Melbourne, I hated the thought of being a long-haul flight away from my family but also couldn't see myself leaving the social circles I'd found in the Southern Hemisphere.

If adolescence is when try on identities before adulthood, maybe commitment phobia is a convenient cubby-hole for TCKs who don't have a heritage as others do. I sometimes envy my Kiwi cousins: New Zealand is in their blood, our family stories, and our grandparents' birth certificates. They sound Kiwi. They have Kiwi memories. They have Kiwi heritage.

For TCKs, on the other hand, we have a constructed heritage. While heritage often implies an *inherited* collective identity, belief system, or gene pool, the Third Culture Kid heritage is mainly psychological and sociological instead of physiological and genetic.

Our heritage exists because our parents' generation created it. Our heritage results from human resourcefulness and wanderlust: the rise of multinational corporations, globalisation, and the technology enabling ubiquitous air travel. We are citizens of the global village.

The fact that we all struggled to find a single, primary culture to wholeheartedly invest in – as we are always on the cusp of multiple cultures – helped me understand why it was so difficult to pick a city in which to settle. I had moved back to New Zealand after university expecting to feel at home, but

I felt more like an outsider than ever. Yet if not New Zealand, where else could I go?

One weekend afternoon browsing Unity Books, my favourite bookstore in Wellington, I stumbled upon Richard Florida's book '*Who's Your City?*'

He talks about how The Biggest Decision of All is where we choose to set our lives. This is the decision that has an equal, if not greater, effect on our economic future, happiness, and overall life outcome. The place we choose to live can determine our income, the people we cross paths with, the friendships we grow, the partners we end up having children with, and the options available to our future families. It is the central life factor that affects how all the others – work, education, and love – follow.

While it's tempting to believe that in today's globalised "flat" world, place is irrelevant, Florida argues that place is more crucial to the global economy than ever before because today's key economic factors (talent, innovation, and creativity) are not evenly distributed across the world, but are concentrated in specific locations. I felt like I had learned more about tech start-ups just from waking up in Wellington instead of Melbourne for the past little while.

He says that many of us lack the mental frameworks to choose where to live, and he talks about a model providing a basic logic for thinking about what we value in our communities. When given a wide range of choices, we need to identify our key needs and priorities and then find a place that meets them at a price we are willing and able to pay. But what if you don't know what your key needs and priorities are just yet?

After all, identity is a process. The self is a construction, and those who have been uprooted as children struggle with the very foundation upon which the rest of their entire life is built. They have been given multiple foundations; multiple options; they craft their unique blueprint as a result. They don't struggle with settling into new places – they struggle with knowing where to ultimately return.

I was starting to learn that part of becoming an adult TCK is selecting the part of yourself you want to amplify. When I weighed up which continent I wanted to base myself in, I was considering my Asian self, my Western self, the part of me that loved the intellectual energy of big cities, the other part of me that valued the spiritual salve of being in the middle of nature.

When dancing between cities or continents, you can have all those parts of yourself peacefully cohabiting inside you. As your life starts to fuse with those around you and decisions start to feel more semi-permanent, you hear the sound of other doors closing, other cultures within you, and other parts of yourself you are deliberately choosing not to ignite.

I bought Richard Florida's book even though I had read the gist of it in the bookstore. It sat on my shelf for months. After skimming it, I was afraid of the questions I was starting to ask.

[10]

10,000 HOURS

*"If it is right, it happens — The main thing is not to hurry.
Nothing good gets away."*

\- JOHN STEINBECK

AT THE START OF 2009, London kept coming up in conversations. My brother, who I missed a lot, had moved there for university, and I was hearing about his experiences via Skype, long emails and the landline (this was life pre-Whatsapp). My parents had gone to visit him, and hearing about their trip – like how they'd met up in London with some friends from Hong Kong for a Thai lunch – made something in my stomach twist with jealousy. London sounded so cosmopolitan, and now that my brother was over there, it felt less like a faraway place and more like a new city we were adding to the Hong Kong–Malaysia–New Zealand culture triangle of our family.

Chase was planning to go to London for his 'OE' (for Kiwis, the 'Overseas Experience' is like a two-year Gap Year that people do in their twenties before coming back to New Zealand to settle down). The more we heard about friends and colleagues of his who had moved over there, the more it became a real possibility for us to explore.

All of this made me want to find out whether I could even live in London with my New Zealand passport. I started looking up options and came across the Youth Mobility Visa, which would guarantee at least my first couple of years in the UK. Then I would start looking up different university websites. I was considering law school. Then in the middle of searching, I would get to a certain point and stop and shut down all the windows.

Was I just running away again? Was this restlessness something I would ever control? In *Belonging Everywhere & Nowhere*, marriage and family therapist Lois Bushong outlines that inner turmoil: the constant urge to move to a new location, to change jobs, to have 'an internal clock that has no idea how to stay in one place more than a couple of years'.

Even if I was aware of my TCK tendencies, that didn't mean I wanted to obey them without questioning them. Maybe it was time to put an end to all the running. After all, things finally felt more familiar in Wellington. I had moved in with Sue and her boyfriend, and Chase and I were happy in our routine. Chase's parents had welcomed me to their family with open arms. His Mum and I now had a weekly ritual of watching *Desperate Housewives* together every Monday night in their living room after dinner. yMedia was ticking along, and we'd just had two more business partners join the venture, who had given it new energy and clarity.

When it came to settling into Wellington, I thought about the 10,000-hour rule. Popularised by Malcolm Gladwell as "the magic number of greatness", he talks about how for anyone to excel, they have to devote that many quality practice hours to their craft. Whether playing the violin or learning computer programming, apparently it takes that many hours of intensive practice to achieve mastery. Gladwell explains how the crux to reaching genuine expertise is a matter of practising, *in the correct way*, for a minimum of that time.

"Achievement is talent plus preparation," he writes in *Outliers*. "The problem with this view is that the closer psychologists look at the careers of the gifted, the smaller the role innate talent seems to play and the bigger role preparation seems to play."

He mentions that practice unlocks 'practical intelligence' (or street smarts). Originally a term from Robert Strunberg, it describes the ability that some people have to find "an optimal fit between themselves and the demands of the environment through adapting, shaping, or selecting a new environment in the pursuit of personally valued goals."

I realised these concepts could also apply to how much 'expertise' or 'practical intelligence' we feel in more personal areas: the places in which we live, the people we love, the friends we learn. The 10,000 hour idea – and the link that it had to developing practical intelligence - could be linked to how 'at home' we feel with the cities and people we choose. The high-quality practice Gladwell refers to could be translated as quality time generally.

The figure translates to just over thirteen and a half months. Perhaps it takes 10,000 hours to fully transition from Friday night love into Tuesday night love. Or 10,000 hours to decide if someone is a true friend. It took us 10,000 hours to grow yMedia into a viable venture. And maybe it takes 10,000 hours to build a support system. Maybe it takes even longer to really create a life in a city and to pour yourself into a community and identity that grounds you.

The hard thing is figuring out what we want to spend that amount of time on, because just reaching it takes such patience and dedication. As a TCK, you can't possibly take all the potential avenues you can envision because you don't have an unlimited amount of hours to put thousands into one city where you might feel at home and thousands into another.

At that point, I hadn't given Wellington the full 10,000 hours, and part of me wanted to see what would happen if I did. Yet another part of me was aching to get out into the broader world and see more of it. Therapy hadn't given me the answers. It had just taught me to sit with the questions instead of trying to fast-forward through them.

When I was thirteen, and before we left Hong Kong, I was talking to a friend on the phone about moving to Auckland. I remember twirling the landline cord and telling her I was trying to look forward to it. By then, I had given up the fight to try and convince my headmistress to block the metaphorical bulldozers with me. The bulldozer was coming, so I might as well brace myself.

"Are you nervous?" Suki asked.

"Not really," I lied.

"Really?"

"Well, a little," I confessed. "It's making friends that's going to be hard."

"You know, I'm sure on your first day, I can see you waiting in the parking lot for your Mum to pick you up, and you'll bond with someone about liking drama, and you'll become friends like that," she said.

It was such a tiny moment that I'm sure she doesn't remember now, but I continued to think about it for years to come. I held onto that promise, that reassurance, and I used it as a way to try and settle into everywhere I ended up living afterwards.

Drama friends didn't happen on the first day of high school. I quickly made friends with whom I could compare our classes and things that annoyed us about certain teachers. But it took ages to make real friends with whom I could analyse crushes and things that annoyed us about our parents.

Yet Suki was right about some of it. As a teenager, I began to feel connected to Auckland when I started doing what had made me feel most like myself in Hong Kong – I started a student newspaper, took part in drama productions, and became close with classmates who had also been raised in international schools.

It taught me that interests matter. Shared interests matter. And what I was starting to realise, thanks to Richard Florida's book, is that your physical base can determine the extent to which you enable yourself to follow your deepest interests. Much like moving to Wellington had allowed Pam and I to focus on yMedia, maybe it was time to think about where the best place was to keep growing professionally for the years ahead. Would somewhere like London, New York or San Francisco offer something I couldn't find in Wellington?

While I had thought moving back to New Zealand would help me commit to my identity as a Kiwi, I had learned that the only identity I would ever feel comfortable committing to was that of a TCK. The more new friends I made in Wellington, the more I noticed that the ones I connected with most deeply were those with international curiosity: they'd travelled, they wanted to travel, and they wanted to experience life beyond New Zealand.

It didn't take a full 10,000 hours to build the kind of bond where you could intuitively understand each other or automatically and easily feel comfortable in silence. Yet it always seemed to take a while in a new city to find friends with whom you wanted to spend even a hundred hours around in the first place.

One day when I was back in Hong Kong visiting for Christmas in 2008, I asked Dad what he thought about where I should base myself. We ate chicken sandwiches in the restaurant underneath his office, and I casually tried to sneak the question into the conversation.

"What would you do if, uh, you were me?" I asked him.

I caught him mid-bite, and he kept chewing. And chewing. That silence felt like two hours instead of five seconds.

"I'd think beyond New Zealand," he said carefully. "It will always be there. If you're ever going to move to London, this is probably the best time."

He said something else that stuck with me. "It's a big decision. And the important thing is to really, really take your time making a big decision. Don't rush it. But once you've made it, don't look back; don't waste your time wondering what could have happened because it's a waste of time to do that."

I felt like all I had been doing for most of the past year was exactly what he said not to do: overthinking this decision of where to live after university. I'd chosen Wellington at first, but was it too late to change my answer to London?

[11]

MULTI-CHOICE TESTS

"Home need not always be a place. It can be a territory, a relationship, a craft, a way of expression. Home is an experience of belonging, a feeling of being whole and known, sometimes too close for comfort. It's those attachments that liberate us more than they constrain. As the expression suggests, home is where we are from — the place where we begin to be."

\- GIANPIERO PETRIGLIERI

THE DECISION TO MOVE TO London didn't happen overnight, nor did the decision to apply to law school. Instead, it was more of a curiosity that I chose to follow instead of ignoring. I sent off my application to law school in London and decided that if I got in, that would be a sign that I should go there and live with my brother.

When I told Pam, she was supportive and was considering moving to Vancouver herself. Maybe Wellington had been a chapter we had needed before we went to wherever we were meant to land next. After all, the two business partners who had joined yMedia had taken what Pam and I had created and made it into something even bigger.

With fresh eyes and new energy, they were signing up new sponsors, releasing new materials, and creating new processes that made everything so much better. They were also based in Auckland, and yMedia was starting to outgrow us, which is what any founder wants, even if it made me feel how I imagine Mum felt the first time I chose to hang out with friends instead of her.

Pam and I had come to Wellington to grow yMedia, but if it no longer needed us, was there any real reason to stay? I had seen that a new city could sometimes be the best place to let go of old regrets. For me, Wellington was where I let go of a lot of the unresolved grief I hadn't realised I had been carrying around as a TCK, which had been triggered by Dane.

Although as time passed with Chase, I saw that perhaps everything that happened with Dane was some kind of practice run. Like Curtis Sittenfeld said, "There are people we treat wrong and later we're prepared to treat other people right. Perhaps this sounds mercenary, but I feel grateful for these trial relationships, and I would like to think it all evens out - surely, unknowingly, I have served as practice for other people."

I still regretted how some part of my brain had interpreted a potential relationship with Dane and twisted it into an emotional death sentence. But after meeting Chase, I was also more convinced that our early twenties was when we were all *meant* to see what fit instead of assuming the theories we held about what we wanted were accurate.

After all, as TCKs become adults, those experiments are what allow us to figure out where we want to land. Wellington had made me reevaluate my relationship with wanderlust, especially in an age of individualisation and globalisation. Every time we studied the two concepts in sociology at university, I noticed how much they were linked. The more globalised we become, the more individualised we become.

TCKs are hyper-globalised and also hyper-individualised. We have seen so much of the world, but that is what creates a new type of solitude. This is what I was starting to see was part of the permanent package of being a TCK. I was also starting to see that solitude didn't need to mean loneliness. You could be the only one who fully understand your own culture, but you could also still build deep emotional connections to others.

Also – after being with Chase, who had grown up in Wellington and was fully Kiwi, I saw that he too wrestled with whether or not to go to London, when to go, and how long he should plan to be away. I was accepting that these major life decisions on where to live and who to be with were part of any millennial's journey.

TCKs are not the only ones struggling to decide where and how to belong - these issues are part of the zeitgeist, as identity is more fluid than ever. Even those who have had stable up-bringings rooted in one city and culture have less solid answers regarding where they will live in five years.

I also knew that it could be hard to talk about with parents, but that was okay. Maybe growing up just meant learning to make your own mind up about things. Plus our parents came of age in a totally different world. For our Boomer parents, the question of belonging was answered much earlier – the early twenties were about picking a partner and career and settling with your choices.

For millennials, our twenties had become twilight years: makeshift tribes, job-hopping, and the search for love were rites of passages before making permanent commitments. Sociologists call it emerging adulthood, where we have bonus adolescence time and more freedom to test-drive potential alternative endings before we sit down to write this thing.

This means that our mash-up life stories can be arranged in whatever city we choose – the "right" path isn't so clear anymore. We're now accustomed to customised narratives – we can choose the elements we want to include in building our identities instead of having those collective narratives spelt out for us.

It can be as overwhelming as it is liberating and sometimes means that we end up putting off important choices for as long as possible, as *The Defining Decade*, by clinical psychologist Meg Jay explores. She talks about how the twenties are often misconstrued as a disposable decade. Instead, she argues, you make the most important decisions during this decade.

The twenties, she argues, set the foundation for an adult life. She says that the two most important choices you make – who you marry (or don't) and what you choose to do for work – are the ones you answer during this decade through the habits and behaviours you set for yourself.

As a TCK reading this book, it only put more pressure on me to figure out things that I felt like I was still finding out. Even after therapy, sometimes I still felt like in my head, I was operating on one of those screens in the *Minority Report* movie, calculating a million different scenarios like Tom Cruise's character and trying to make the choice that feels best. When I tried to settle on a single answer around career or where I should live, my head was just as full of spaghetti as it had always been, even though I now had better tools to sort it out.

I was still nervous about making commitments even though I knew I had to get over that in order to grow up. I saw that a commitment is simply a chosen constraint and that this is what *The Defining Decade* was talking about: choosing your constraints instead of endlessly floating around in circles. I thought deciding where to call home would be the ultimate factor in helping me figure out all the rest. Yet I kept getting tripped up when I felt I had to pick just one identity.

I was finding that the TCK lifestyle is about coming to terms with the concept of "both" as opposed to "either/or" – "either/or" will drive you crazy; "both" will make you grateful.

This year in a brand new city, full of introductions to unfamiliar faces, and meeting new people through yMedia, had taught me that I was not from Hong Kong *or* New Zealand. I was not fully Malaysian *or* Kiwi. Like my brother, I was from all those places. I was from *both* Hong Kong *and* New Zealand.

I had seen from a young age that everything had a price: you pay for security through sacrificing freedom, you pay for depth by sacrificing wanderlust. You pay for expat life by sacrificing the feeling of being a local. When you've got multiple environments in which to base the context of your life, you can become unusually immune to the opinions of your peers and a single local environment.

Learning to melt this immunity is what I had gained in this past year. Not being affected by anyone else means that you don't need anyone. And if you go through life convinced you don't need anyone, then you teach others not to need you either. If you keep thinking you can just hop from city to city, forever unattached, you don't let a city become part of who you are.

Yet even though I saw that there would never be a single, mystical place that would be 'home', I felt a strong pull to London that grew stronger over time. There are simply the places we end up choosing and the choices we make in those places about how long we stay and why. Embracing this took away pressure I had previously put on myself to 'pick' the 'right' place to call home. What I have come to learn is that there is no such thing.

I'd learned that for TCKs, home keeps moving. What defines TCKs is our cultural marginality. As Nagesh Rao put it: "They do not fit perfectly into any specific culture where they have lived, but on the other hand, fit comfortably on the edge or margin of any one of them. In essence, they feel at home anywhere and nowhere at the same time."

For as long as I could remember, I had been trying to find my way back to a place I never knew. It was only in the past year that I had seen this as something I could be celebrating, not struggling with; being slightly anchorless could be liberating as opposed to tragic.

To celebrate the core of being a Third Culture Kid is to embrace impermanence and to recognise that nothing in life is ever truly fixed; whether it's a person or a place, nothing belongs to us and could fade tomorrow. We can have multiple universes and lives within us and simultaneously belong to all and none of them. It took years to realise that this transient multiplicity wasn't something I needed to run away from.

I could choose to embrace a global culture instead of feeling like I didn't fully relate to any. Finding a place to call home wasn't about passing or failing a multi-choice test. It was about accepting that as a TCK, I was a walking multi-choice test and always would be. Being a TCK was my identity, and the world was my home. Commitment was a practice that I was still learning, outgrowing the need to run from place to place in search of something that could never be defined.

[12]

AIRPORTS

*"The only thing we never get enough of is love;
and the only thing we never give enough of is love."*

HENRY MILLER

BEFORE I LEFT WELLINGTON, I had a final in-person session with Annette in the room that I had come to know so well. As I glanced at what was now familiar art on the walls, I told her about this weird mixture of feelings that were bubbling up as I prepared to leave the city.

"You have begun a bit of a grieving process," she said.

After all the sessions we had done exploring the grief rollercoaster that can come with moving around, I felt better equipped to handle whatever came next. I had found that the more I could let myself feel the sadness that inevitably came with goodbyes, the more I could open myself up to *all* feelings – including the joys of discovering a new place.

"The world truly becomes global when we can go and live in whichever part of the world we like without time restrictions," she said. "It's a wee while till we get to that point yet, and you are one of the pioneers."

I didn't feel like a pioneer. I felt nervous and excited about going to London, but now that I had gone through the move to Wellington, I felt more equipped to face whatever came next.

After all, maybe it was here that I had learned what being a TCK was really all about. I used to question if being a TCK was a fundamentally unnatural thing. As humans, maybe we're not designed to ingest that many different cultural experiences and transitions in such a short timeframe, especially during childhood. We can get cultural indigestion, feel psychologically claustrophobic in non-global cultures, and experience too much subconscious grief at too young an age.

Yet we also develop this tightly defined individuality, this ability to carry a life in a literal and emotional suitcase. In that difference comes a confinement, and maybe being a Third Culture Kid makes you want to outrun a fear of being forgotten. Everyone else got a nationality or some marker of an original tribe; we didn't. Perhaps being a Third Culture Kid is about building a life where we prevent that 'outsider' feeling from ever happening to us again.

After all, now – after therapy – when I looked back on how I had 'done' throughout school, I saw much more to it than I had originally thought. I now saw an overachiever – the kind of girl who later grows up to be a workaholic. I now saw someone who stayed busy to escape the pain of losing everything that had once been familiar, who pushed away anyone who tried to get too close in case she had to lose them again. I saw someone scared of getting too attached to anyone who would pin her down and make her live in a city she didn't want to live in.

Maybe being a TCK was about more than being 'the friend who's from everywhere' or 'the girl who grew up all over the place'. Maybe it was about being born into a global neighbour-hood, having wanderlust in your emotional DNA, and having that overcomplicate your psychological GPS. Therapy taught me to create my own unique system of values, borrowing parts of each culture and finding a system that worked for me as an individual.

It also taught me to explore frameworks that helped the world make more sense to me. One of the final concepts I kept thinking about was something that researcher Dr Greg Madison calls existential migration, which is the best way I could describe why I decided to move to London.

In his online explanation of existential migration, Dr Madison talks about how economic migration is when someone leaves their country of origin purely for economic reasons: a better job, better wages, and so on. Wanderlust is when someone has a strong desire to travel simply for the sake of it. 'Existential migration' is when someone is expressing 'something funda-mental about personal existence by leaving one's homeland and becoming a foreigner'.

According to Dr Madison, 'home' can be 'interaction' instead of being a geographical place, with the 'self' being "actively created in interaction with one's surroundings" with the environment either building or blocking the development of potential. I loved this idea as it summed up exactly why I had chosen to study in Melbourne over Auckland University, why I wanted to move back to New Zealand, and why so many of my friends were taking up job offers and opportunities around the world.

We wanted to become somebody we didn't think we could become in the places we were based. It was the move that would allow us to become the people we knew we could be. Being in the new city would allow us to take up opportunities that just weren't available in the place of origin. We weren't being driven out of our countries through war, famine or persecution, we were being pulled towards new places by hopes and dreams of becoming better versions of ourselves.

It's a privilege to be able to make that choice. The classes I had done in Melbourne and the lecturers I had studied with just weren't available in Auckland. yMedia just wasn't available in Australia. Had I become a better person? It was hard to tell. I know that I'd been challenged in a way that I wouldn't have been if I had stayed still.

I wasn't moving London just to go to law school and live with my brother. I was moving there to become someone I didn't think that I could be if I stayed in New Zealand.

In September 2009, around the 10,000-hour mark of when I'd first moved to Wellington, I headed up to Auckland for my flight to London. Pam was catching her flight to Vancouver on the same evening. The two business partners who took over yMedia saw us off at Auckland Airport. It felt like being dropped off at secondary school for the first time all over again, except we weren't going to get to reunite after the school day was over.

"Don't cry because it's over, smile because it happened" wasn't something I could bring myself to say. But I felt in the airport that evening that everything that had brought us to this point had *meant* to happen. I couldn't describe why but I could tell the others felt a similar mix of emotions to me: happiness that we'd met, sadness that we were scattering, gratitude for everything that we had collectively built over the past year, excitement about what was going to come next.

We all had a quick dinner together in the area before security, as Pam and I double-checked our boarding passes. Before we walked through security, the four of us embraced in a group hug. We also took a photo – not on our phones at the time (this was the pre-selfie era) – but from asking a passerby to use Pam's camera.

Flying out of New Zealand with Pam on that last night felt strangely poetic. We were heading to different corners of the world and would be further apart than ever, but in some ways, it felt like it was time. She helped me understand parts of myself that I had previously ignored and we had our own version of a great love story. Like any great love story, I knew that there were future chapters ahead, but for now it felt like we both needed some space and time to figure out who we were again after yMedia.

Over the past year, I had seen that as a kid, you build your life in each new place when you're a TCK. You get dropped into foreign cultures; you have to simultaneously figure out how to navigate while retaining the part of yourself that is independent of any culture or nation. You figure out how much of the past you want to keep and how much of the future you will include in your relationship with this place.

As an adult TCK, you have to figure out how much of that way of living you want to take with you into your future. Do you want to be in motion forever or do you want to learn to stand still? The question I struggled with in my first few months back in New Zealand after university was: is this it? That led to other questions: if this isn't home, then where to next? When I'm done moving, where will I stop? Will I ever?

I can now see that I was wrestling with commitment, and I am not the first and last TCK to deal with this. I learned in Wellington that the TCK's predisposition to commitment phobia is only logical, to some extent. If you've learned you can lose an entire world in just one plane ride, at an age when you're not old enough to conceptualise not *everything* you love will always be lost, you're bound to be wary when it comes to deep attachments.

I spent years searching for ways to connect to something I had no idea I had lost while growing up. I started to find it through yMedia, Pam, Annette, Chase, everyone I met in the windy capital city of my passport country. Yet the way I started to find my way home was, paradoxically, to accept that what I was looking for was never going to be a place or a person. Instead, it was a feeling. If there's one thing I took away from those sessions with Annette, it was that the iron heart feels nothing and the open heart feels everything.

Home can be a place within yourself, and the more aligned your actions and behaviours are to that place, the bigger a web you can create around yourself – an environment, a social life, an ecosystem that resonates and aligns with home. Home is where you're not lonely. You can be by yourself and feel at home, or in a crowded room and feel completely invisible.

It's about how visible you feel in your own life, in your own skin. I had seen that the world, rather than one city, could be my home. It did not have to be limited to a place on the map. Instead, it could be a feeling I carried around wherever I went.

EPILOGUE

I STARTED WRITING ABOUT HOME BUT ended up talking about love because both are about belonging. Maybe there are no 'right' or 'wrong' people or places. The people we love, like the places we choose to live in, are simply reflections of something more internal, patterns we may not even become consciously aware of until years later.

In therapy I had learned that coming home to yourself is a process. The difference with being a TCK is that home is something you have the chance to consciously create, more proactively than the person who is born knowing which national anthem speaks to their blood and which spot on a map marks their emotional centre of gravity.

When you're a TCK, your national anthem is a mash-up of others; your emotional centre of gravity is global. You are a cultural orphan; the cultures you adopt are just that – 'adopted'. In the darkest moments, your sense of belonging can feel manufactured as opposed to organic, as if something essential floats just beyond your reach, outside of you instead of inside you.

For TCKs, the question of home haunts you from an early age – its complexity, its elusive nature, its promise. I thought I would have clearer answers by the time I'd finished writing this piece; instead, I just learned to ask better questions.

Over the years, I stayed in touch with Annette, and we had online video calls that continued to help me while I settled into London. Someone I had once been so terrified to meet turned out to be someone who made a profound difference in my life. People think therapy can be overly indulgent, and too much of it can be. But for me, it not only changed my life for the better, but it also helped to change the lives of my friends, who had their own questions to face around work, relationships, family issues, and where to go next.

As the years went on, I kept encouraging friends to seek therapy when they were at a crossroads. We can vent to friends and loved ones as much as we want, but ultimately, we are all walking around with our own biases. Therapy is a neutral space. At its best, it's an exercise in calling yourself out on the habits or patterns that no longer serve you to become a stronger version of yourself.

Still, no matter how much of a cheerleader for therapy I was trying so hard to be, sometimes I could see in friends' eyes that the same *Jaws* theme was playing in their minds. And that's fine. For me, therapy taught me what home meant. It taught me that knowing *where* home is means knowing *what* home is. When you've grown up as a TCK, home is an answer you construct, not one you inherit.

When I stopped trying to solve my own 'home' question like a Rubik's Cube and started to view it like a cryptic poem, and I gave up trying to classify what the word meant, the meaning of it began to make sense. It was like a problem that seems impossible until you let yourself forget about it, and then five days later, the answer comes to you in the shower.

REFERENCES & TCK RESOURCES

Are We Caught between Two or More Cultures? The Importance of Teaching Cultural Marginality in Our Classrooms, by Nagesh Rao: https://files.eric.ed.gov/fulltext/ED393145.pdf

A Quantitative Comparison of Young Adult "Third Culture Kids'" Social, Emotional, and Behavioral Health to Peers Who Never Lived Abroad, by Emily Ann Brewer: https://oaktrust.library.tamu.edu/handle/1969.1/188987

Confused or multicultural: Third culture individuals' cultural identity, by Andrea Moore and Gina Barker: https://www.researchgate.net/publication/256976526_Confused_or_multicultural_Third_culture_individuals'_cultural_identity

The Defining Decade: Why Your Twenties Matter--And How to Make the Most of Them Now, by Meg Jay

Depression rates among Third Culture Kids in an international school setting, by Jeffery A Devens: https://www.proquest.com/openview/8bc2eff5d01b5b09fc9bfa088f65969d/1?pq-origsite=gscholar&cbl=18750&diss=y

Denizen: for third culture kids: https://denizenmag.com/

Deresiewicz, William. "Solitude and Leadership." The American Scholar, 1 Mar. 2010, theamericanscholar.org/solitude-and-leadership/.

Existential migration and not 'being-at-home' in the world by Greg Madison:
https://www.gregmadison.net/existential-migration/

He's Scared, She's Scared by Steven Carter and Julia Sokol

Loss and Grief between and Among Cultures: The Experience of Third Culture Kids, by Kathleen R. Gilbert: https://journals.sagepub.com/doi/abs/10.2190/IL.16.2.a

Men Who Can't Love by Steven Carter

Narratives of Third Culture Kids: Commitment and Reticence in Social Relationships, by Anastasia Aldelina Lijadi and Gertina J. van Schalkwyk:
https://www.academia.edu/7723411/
Narratives_of_Third_Culture_Kids_Commitment_
and_Reticence_in_Social_Relationships

Outliers: The Story of Success by Malcolm Gladwell

Reinventing Your Life: The Breakthrough Program to End Negative Behaviour...and Feel Great Again by Janet S. Klosko and Jeffrey Young

Third Culture Kids: Factors that Predict Psychological Health after Repatriation, by Laila Plamondon:
https://scholarworks.smith.edu/theses/1412/

The 7 Habits of Highly Effective Teens Book by Sean Covey

Third Culture Kids: The Experience of Growing Up Among Worlds by David C. Pollock, Ruth E. Van Reken, et al.

TCKs Experience Prolonged Adolescence by Ann Baker Cottrell and Ruth Hill Useem:
http://www.tckworld.com/useem/art3.html

ACKNOWLEDGEMENTS

I first started writing this in London in 2013, and I am grateful to Susannah and Simon Yule and Jack Kuecker for encouraging the idea. I sent the first draft to Pamela Minett, who even from oceans away, has always been so supportive. She mentioned it at a Seattle BBQ to Mallory MacDonald and Emily Copple, who gave feedback on the early version and, better yet, became close friends over time. Thanks to Ivan Cruz for the cover design and to Steph Yiu and Matt Trinetti for their editing and creative partnership.

ABOUT THE AUTHOR

Adele Barlow has written for TCK magazine *Denizen* and *The Huffington Post*, among other publications. Having grown up in Hong Kong, New Zealand, Malaysia and Australia, she now lives in London.

She is the founder of Copy & Co, a boutique content studio serving tech scaleups, investors and agencies in London, New York and Asia. She has spent over a decade leading comms, content and campaigns in the B2C and B2B tech space, including the UK's first Women in Software Power List. She is the author of multiple books.

Website: www.adelebarlow.com

Instagram: @MsAdeleBarlow